Terence Rattigan

AFTER
THE DANCE

Introduced by
DAN REBELLATO

NICK HERN BOOKS
London

www.nickhernbooks.co.uk

A Nick Hern Book

This edition of *After the Dance* first published in Great Britain in 1995 as a paperback original by Nick Hern Books Limited, The Glasshouse, 49a Goldhawk Road, London W12 8QP. *After the Dance* was first published in 1939 by Hamish Hamilton

Reprinted 2002, 2004, 2007, 2008 (twice), 2010

Reprinted in this revised edition 2010, 2011 (twice), 2012, 2014

Copyright © Trustees of the Terence Rattigan Trust 1939
Introduction copyright © 1995, 2010 Dan Rebellato

Front cover photo copyright © Hulton Deutsch Collection

Typeset by Country Setting, Kingsdown, Kent CT14 8ES
Printed in the UK by CPI Group (UK) Ltd

A CIP catalogue record for this book is available from the British Library

ISBN 978 1 85459 217 0

Terence Rattigan

Born in 1911, a scholar at Harrow and at Trinity College, Oxford,
Terence Rattigan had his first long-running hit in the West End
at the age of twenty-five: *French Without Tears* (1936). His next
play, *After the Dance* (1939), opened to euphoric reviews yet
closed under the gathering clouds of war, but with *Flare Path*
(1942) Rattigan embarked on an almost unbroken series of
successes, with most plays running in the West End for at least a
year and several making the transition to Broadway: *While the Sun
Shines* (1943), *Love in Idleness* (1944), *The Winslow Boy* (1946),
The Browning Version (performed in double-bill with
Harlequinade, 1948), *Who is Sylvia?* (1950), *The Deep Blue Sea*
(1952), *The Sleeping Prince* (1953) and *Separate Tables* (1954).
From the mid-fifties, with the advent of the 'Angry Young Men',
he enjoyed less success on stage, though *Ross* (1960) and *In
Praise of Love* (1973) were well received. As well as seeing many
of his plays turned into successful films, Rattigan wrote a number
of original plays for television from the fifties onwards. He was
knighted in 1971 and died in 1977.

Other titles by the same author
published by Nick Hern Books

The Browning Version and *Harlequinade*

Cause Célèbre

The Deep Blue Sea

First Episode

Flare Path

French Without Tears

In Praise of Love

Love in Idleness / *Less Than Kind*

Rattigan's Nijinsky
    (adapted from Rattigan's screenplay by Nicholas Wright)

Separate Tables

Who is Sylvia? and *Duologue*

The Winslow Boy

Terence Rattigan (1911-1977)

Terence Rattigan stood on the steps of the Royal Court Theatre, on 8 May 1956, after the opening night of John Osborne's *Look Back in Anger*. Asked by a reporter what he thought of the play, he replied, with an uncharacteristic lack of discretion, that it should have been retitled 'Look how unlike Terence Rattigan I'm being.' [1] And he was right. The great shifts in British theatre, marked by Osborne's famous première, ushered in kinds of playwriting which were specifically unlike Rattigan's work. The pre-eminence of playwriting as a formal craft, the subtle tracing of the emotional lives of the middle classes – those techniques which Rattigan so perfected – fell dramatically out of favour, creating a veil of prejudice through which his work even now struggles to be seen.

Terence Mervyn Rattigan was born on 10 June 1911, a wet Saturday a few days before George V's coronation. His father, Frank, was in the diplomatic corps and Terry's parents were often posted abroad, leaving him to be raised by his paternal grandmother. Frank Rattigan was a geographically and emotionally distant man, who pursued a string of little-disguised affairs throughout his marriage. Rattigan would later draw on these memories when he created Mark St Neots, the bourgeois Casanova of *Who is Sylvia?* Rattigan was much closer to his mother, Vera Rattigan, and they remained close friends until her death in 1971.

Rattigan's parents were not great theatregoers, but Frank Rattigan's brother had married a Gaiety Girl, causing a minor family uproar, and an apocryphal story suggests that the 'indulgent aunt' reported as taking the young Rattigan to the theatre may have been this scandalous relation.[2] And when, in the summer of 1922, his family went to stay in the country cottage of the drama critic Hubert Griffiths, Rattigan avidly worked through his extensive library of playscripts. Terry went to Harrow in 1925, and there maintained both his somewhat illicit theatregoing habit and his insatiable reading, reputedly devouring every play in the school library. Apart from contemporary authors like Galsworthy, Shaw and Barrie, he also read the plays of Chekhov, a writer whose crucial influence he often acknowledged.[3]

His early attempts at writing, while giving little sign of his later sophistication, do indicate his ability to absorb and reproduce his own theatrical experiences. There was a ten-minute melodrama about the Borgias entitled *The Parchment*, on the cover of which the author recommends with admirable conviction that a suitable cast for this work might comprise 'Godfrey Tearle, Gladys Cooper, Marie Tempest, Matheson Lang, Isobel Elsom, Henry Ainley . . . [and] Noël Coward'.[4] At Harrow, when one of his teachers demanded a French playlet for a composition exercise, Rattigan, undaunted by his linguistic shortcomings, produced a full-throated tragedy of deception, passion and revenge which included the immortal curtain line: 'COMTESSE. (*Souffrant terriblement.*) Non! non! non! Ah non! Mon Dieu, non!'[5] His teacher's now famous response was 'French execrable: theatre sense first class'.[6] A year later, aged fifteen, he wrote *The Pure in Heart,* a rather more substantial play showing a family being pulled apart by a son's crime and the father's desire to maintain his reputation. Rattigan's ambitions were plainly indicated on the title pages, each of which announced the author to be 'the famous playwrite and author T. M. Rattigan.'[7]

Frank Rattigan was less than keen on having a 'playwrite' for a son and was greatly relieved when in 1930, paving the way for a life as a diplomat, Rattigan gained a scholarship to read History at Trinity, Oxford. But Rattigan's interests were entirely elsewhere. A burgeoning political conscience that had led him to oppose the compulsory Officer Training Corps parades at Harrow saw him voice pacifist and socialist arguments at college, even supporting the controversial Oxford Union motion 'This House will in no circumstances fight for its King and Country' in February 1933. The rise of Hitler (which he briefly saw close at hand when he spent some weeks in the Black Forest in July 1933) and the outbreak of the Spanish Civil War saw his radical leanings deepen and intensify. Rattigan never lost his political compassion. After the war he drifted towards the Liberal Party, but he always insisted that he had never voted Conservative, despite the later conception of him as a Tory playwright of the establishment.[8]

Away from the troubled atmosphere of his family, Rattigan began to gain in confidence as the contours of his ambitions and his identity moved more sharply into focus. He soon took advantage of the university's theatrical facilities and traditions. He joined The Oxford Union Dramatic Society (OUDS), where contemporaries included Giles Playfair, George Devine, Peter Glenville, Angus Wilson and Frith Banbury. Each year, OUDS ran a one-act play competition and in Autumn 1931 Rattigan submitted one. Unusually, it seems that this was a highly experimental effort, somewhat like Konstantin's piece in *The Seagull.* George Devine, the OUDS president, apparently told the young author, 'Some of it is absolutely smashing, but it goes too far'.[9] Rattigan was instead to make his first mark as a somewhat scornful reviewer for the student newspaper, *Cherwell*, and as a performer in the Smokers (OUDS's private revue club), where he adopted the persona and dress of 'Lady Diana Coutigan', a drag performance which allowed him to discuss leading members of the Society with a barbed camp wit.[10]

That the name of his Smokers persona echoed the contemporary phrase, 'queer as a coot', indicates Rattigan's new-found confidence in his homosexuality. In February 1932, Rattigan played a tiny part in the OUDS production of *Romeo and Juliet*, which was directed by John Gielgud and starred Peggy Ashcroft and Edith Evans (women undergraduates were not admitted to OUDS, and professional actresses were often recruited). Rattigan's failure to deliver his one line correctly raised an increasingly embarrassing laugh every night (an episode which he re-uses to great effect in *Harlequinade*). However, out of this production came a friendship with Gielgud and his partner, John Perry. Through them, Rattigan was introduced to theatrical and homosexual circles, where his youthful 'school captain' looks were much admired.

A growing confidence in his sexuality and in his writing led to his first major play. In 1931, he shared rooms with a contemporary of his, Philip Heimann, who was having an affair with Irina Basilevich, a mature student. Rattigan's own feelings for Heimann completed an eternal triangle that formed the basis of the play he co-wrote with Heimann, *First Episode*. This play was accepted for production in Surrey's 'Q' theatre; it was respectfully received and subsequently transferred to the Comedy Theatre in London's West End, though carefully shorn of its homosexual subplot. Despite receiving only £50 from this production (and having put £200 into it), Rattigan immediately dropped out of college to become a full-time writer.

Frank Rattigan was displeased by this move, but made a deal with his son. He would give him an allowance of £200 a year for two years and let him live at home to write; if at the end of that period, he had had no discernible success, he would enter a more secure and respectable profession. With this looming deadline, Rattigan wrote quickly. *Black Forest*, an O'Neill-inspired play based on his experiences in Germany in 1933, is one of the three that have survived. Rather unwillingly, he collaborated with Hector Bolitho on an adaptation of the latter's novel, *Grey Farm*, which received a disastrous New York production in 1940. Another project was an adaptation of *A Tale of Two Cities*, written with Gielgud; this fell through at the last minute when Donald Albery, the play's potential producer, received a complaint from actor-manager John Martin-Harvey who was beginning a farewell tour of his own adaptation, *The Only Way*, which he had been performing for forty-five years. As minor compensation, Albery invited Rattigan to send him any other new scripts. Rattigan sent him a play provisionally titled *Gone Away*, based on his experiences in a French language Summer School in 1931. Albery took out a nine-month option on it, but no production appeared.

By mid-1936, Rattigan was despairing. His father had secured him a job with Warner Brothers as an in-house screenwriter, which was reasonably paid; but Rattigan wanted success in the theatre, and his desk-bound life at Teddington Studios seemed unlikely to advance this ambition. By chance, one of Albery's productions was unexpectedly losing money, and the wisest course of action seemed to be to pull the show and replace it with something cheap. Since *Gone Away* required a relatively small cast and only one set, Albery quickly arranged for a production. Harold French, the play's director, had only one qualm: the title. Rattigan suggested *French Without Tears*, which was immediately adopted.

After an appalling dress rehearsal, no one anticipated the rapturous response of the first-night audience, led by Cicely Courtneidge's infectious laugh. The following morning Kay Hammond, the show's female lead, discovered Rattigan surrounded by the next day's reviews. 'But I don't believe it', he said. 'Even *The Times* likes it.' [11]

French Without Tears played over 1000 performances in its three-year run and Rattigan was soon earning £100 a week. He moved out of his father's home, wriggled out of his Warner Brothers contract, and dedicated himself to spending the money as soon as it came in. Partly this was an attempt to defer the moment when he had to follow up this enormous success. In the event, both of his next plays were undermined by the outbreak of war.

After the Dance, an altogether more bleak indictment of the Bright Young Things' failure to engage with the iniquities and miseries of contemporary life, opened, in June 1939, to euphoric reviews; but only a month later the European crisis was darkening the national mood and audiences began to dwindle. The play was pulled in August after only sixty performances. *Follow My Leader* was a satirical farce closely based on the rise of Hitler, co-written with an Oxford contemporary, Tony Goldschmidt (writing as Anthony Maurice in case anyone thought he was German). It suffered an alternative fate. Banned from production in 1938, owing to the Foreign Office's belief that 'the production of this play at this time would not be in the best interests of the country',[12] it finally received its première in 1940, by which time Rattigan and Goldschmidt's mild satire failed to capture the real fears that the war was unleashing in the country.

Rattigan's insecurity about writing now deepened. An interest in Freud, dating back to his Harrow days, encouraged him to visit a psychiatrist that he had known while at Oxford, Dr Keith Newman. Newman exerted a svengali-like influence on Rattigan and persuaded the pacifist playwright to join the RAF as a means of curing his writer's block. Oddly, this unorthodox treatment seemed to have some effect; by 1941, Rattigan was writing again. On one dramatic sea crossing, an engine failed, and with everyone forced to jettison all excess baggage and possessions, Rattigan threw the hard covers and blank pages from the notebook containing his new play, stuffing the precious manuscript into his jacket.

Rattigan drew on his RAF experiences to write a new play, *Flare Path*. Bronson Albery and Bill Linnit who had both supported *French Without Tears* both turned the play down, believing that the last thing that the public wanted was a play about the war.[13] H. M. Tennent Ltd., led by the elegant Hugh 'Binkie' Beaumont, was the third management offered the script; and in 1942, *Flare Path* opened in London, eventually playing almost 700 performances. Meticulously interweaving the stories of three couples against the backdrop of wartime uncertainty, Rattigan found himself 'commended, if not exactly as a professional playwright, at least as a promising apprentice who had definitely begun to learn the rudiments of his job'.[14] Beaumont, already on the way to becoming the most powerful and successful West End producer of the era, was an influential ally for Rattigan. There is a curious side-story to this production; Dr Keith Newman decided to watch 250 performances of this play and write up the insights that his 'serial attendance' had afforded him. George Bernard Shaw remarked that such playgoing behaviour 'would have driven me mad; and I am not sure that [Newman] came out of it without a slight derangement'. Shaw's caution was wise.[15] In late 1945, Newman went insane and eventually died in a psychiatric hospital.

Meanwhile, Rattigan had achieved two more successes; the witty farce, *While the Sun Shines*, and the more serious, though politically clumsy, *Love in Idleness* (retitled *O Mistress Mine* in America). He had also co-written a number of successful films, including *The Day Will Dawn, Uncensored, The Way to the Stars* and an adaptation of *French Without Tears*. By the end of 1944, Rattigan had three plays running in the West End, a record only beaten by Somerset Maugham's four in 1908.

Love in Idleness was dedicated to Henry 'Chips' Channon, the Tory MP who had become Rattigan's lover. Channon's otherwise gossipy diaries record their meeting very discreetly: 'I dined with Juliet Duff in her little flat . . . also there, Sibyl Colefax and Master Terence Rattigan, and we sparkled over the Burgundy. I like Rattigan enormously, and feel a new friendship has begun. He has a flat in Albany'.[16] Tom Driberg's rather less discreet account fleshes out the story: Channon's 'seduction of the playwright was almost like the wooing of Danaë by Zeus – every day the playwright found, delivered to his door, a splendid present – a case of champagne, a huge pot of caviar, a Cartier cigarette-box in two kinds of gold . . . In the end, of course, he gave in, saying apologetically to his friends, 'How can one *not?*' '.[17] It was a very different set in which Rattigan now moved, one that was wealthy and conservative, the very people he had criticised in *After the*

Dance. Rattigan did not share the complacency of many of his friends, and his next play revealed a deepening complexity and ambition.

For a long time, Rattigan had nurtured a desire to become respected as a serious writer; the commercial success of *French Without Tears* had, however, sustained the public image of Rattigan as a wealthy young light comedy writer-about-town. [18] With *The Winslow Boy*, which premièred in 1946, Rattigan began to turn this image around. In doing so he entered a new phase as a playwright. As one contemporary critic observed, this play 'put him at once into the class of the serious and distinguished writer'.[19] The play, based on the Archer-Shee case in which a family attempted to sue the Admiralty for a false accusation of theft against their son, featured some of Rattigan's most elegantly crafted and subtle characterization yet. The famous second curtain, when the barrister Robert Morton subjects Ronnie Winslow to a vicious interrogation before announcing that 'The boy is plainly innocent. I accept the brief', brought a joyous standing ovation on the first night. No less impressive is the subtle handling of the concept of 'justice' and 'rights' through the play of ironies which pits Morton's liberal complacency against Catherine Winslow's feminist convictions.

Two years later, Rattigan's *Playbill*, comprising the one-act plays *The Browning Version* and *Harlequinade*, showed an ever deepening talent. The latter is a witty satire of the kind of touring theatre encouraged by the new Committee for the Encouragement of Music and Arts (CEMA, the immediate forerunner of the Arts Council). But the former's depiction of a failed, repressed Classics teacher evinced an ability to choreograph emotional subtleties on stage that outstripped anything Rattigan had yet demonstrated.

Adventure Story, which in 1949 followed hard on the heels of *Playbill*, was less successful. An attempt to dramatize the emotional dilemmas of Alexander the Great, Rattigan seemed unable to escape the vernacular of his own circle, and the epic scheme of the play sat oddly with Alexander's more prosaic concerns.

Rattigan's response to both the critical bludgeoning of this play and the distinctly luke-warm reception of *Playbill* on Broadway was to write a somewhat extravagant article for the *New Statesman*. 'Concerning the Play of Ideas' was a desire to defend the place of 'character' against those who would insist on the pre-eminence in drama of ideas.[20] The essay is not clear and is couched in such teasing terms that it is at first difficult to see why it should have secured such a fervent response. James Bridie, Benn Levy, Peter Ustinov, Sean O'Casey, Ted Willis, Christopher Fry and finally George Bernard Shaw all weighed in to support or condemn the article. Finally Rattigan replied in slightly more moderate

terms to these criticisms insisting (and the first essay reasonably
supports this) that he was not calling for the end of ideas in the
theatre, but rather for their inflection through character and
situation.[21] However, the damage was done (as, two years later,
with his 'Aunt Edna', it would again be done). Rattigan was
increasingly being seen as the arch-proponent of commercial
vacuity.[22]

The play Rattigan had running at the time added weight to his
opponents' charge. Originally planned as a dark comedy, *Who is
Sylvia?* became a rather more frivolous thing both in the writing
and the playing. Rattled by the failure of *Adventure Story*, and
superstitiously aware that the new play was opening at the
Criterion, where fourteen years before *French Without Tears* had
been so successful, Rattigan and everyone involved in the
production had steered it towards light farce and obliterated the
residual seriousness of the original conceit.

Rattigan had ended his affair with Henry Channon and taken
up with Kenneth Morgan, a young actor who had appeared in
Follow My Leader and the film of *French Without Tears*. However,
the relationship had not lasted and Morgan had for a while been
seeing someone else. Rattigan's distress was compounded one day
in February 1949, when he received a message that Morgan had
killed himself. Although horrified, Rattigan soon began to
conceive an idea for a play. Initially it was to have concerned a
homosexual relationship, but Beaumont, his producer, persuaded
him to change the relationship to a heterosexual one.[23] At a time
when the Lord Chamberlain refused to allow any plays to be
staged that featured homosexuality, such a proposition would have
been a commercial impossibility. The result is one of the finest
examples of Rattigan's craft. The story of Hester Collyer, trapped
in a relationship with a man incapable of returning her love, and
her transition from attempted suicide to groping, uncertain self-
determination is handled with extraordinary economy, precision
and power. The depths of despair and desire that Rattigan plumbs
have made *The Deep Blue Sea* one of his most popular and
moving pieces.

1953 saw Rattigan's romantic comedy *The Sleeping Prince*, planned
as a modest, if belated, contribution to the Coronation festivities.
However, the project was hypertrophied by the insistent presence of
Laurence Olivier and Vivien Leigh in the cast and the critics were
disturbed to see such whimsy from the author of *The Deep Blue Sea*.

Two weeks after its opening, the first two volumes of Rattigan's
Collected Plays were published. The preface to the second volume
introduced one of Rattigan's best-known, and most notorious
creations: Aunt Edna. 'Let us invent,' he writes, 'a character, a
nice respectable, middle-class, middle-aged, maiden lady, with
time on her hands and the money to help her pass it'.[24] Rattigan

paints a picture of this eternal theatregoer, whose bewildered disdain for modernism ('Picasso—'those dreadful reds, my dear, and why three noses?'')[25] make up part of the particular challenge of dramatic writing. The intertwined commercial and cultural pressures that the audience brings with it exert considerable force on the playwright's work.

Rattigan's creation brought considerable scorn upon his head. But Rattigan is neither patronizing nor genuflecting towards Aunt Edna. The whole essay is aimed at demonstrating the crucial rôle of the audience in the theatrical experience. Rattigan's own sense of theatre was *learned* as a member of the audience, and he refuses to distance himself from this woman: 'despite my already self-acknowledged creative ambitions I did not in the least feel myself a being apart. If my neighbours gasped with fear for the heroine when she was confronted with a fate worse than death, I gasped with them'.[26] But equally, he sees his job as a writer to engage in a gentle tug-of-war with the audience's expectations: 'although Aunt Edna must never be made mock of, or bored, or befuddled, she must equally not be wooed, or pandered to or cosseted'.[27] The complicated relation between satisfying and surprising this figure may seem contradictory, but as Rattigan notes, 'Aunt Edna herself is indeed a highly contradictory character'.[28]

But Rattigan's argument, as in the 'Play of Ideas' debate before it, was taken to imply an insipid pandering to the unchallenging expectations of his audience. Aunt Edna dogged his career from that moment on and she became such a by-word for what theatre should *not* be that in 1960, the Questors Theatre, Ealing, could title a triple-bill of Absurdist plays, 'Not For Aunt Edna'.[29]

Rattigan's next play did help to restore his reputation as a serious dramatist. *Separate Tables* was another double-bill, set in a small Bournemouth hotel. The first play develops Rattigan's familiar themes of sexual longing and humiliation while the second pits a man found guilty of interfering with women in a local cinema against the self-appointed moral jurors in the hotel. The evening was highly acclaimed and the subsequent Broadway production a rare American success.

However, Rattigan's reign as the leading British playwright was about to be brought to an abrupt end. In a car from Stratford to London, early in 1956, Rattigan spent two and a half hours informing his Oxford contemporary George Devine why the new play he had discovered would not work in the theatre. When Devine persisted, Rattigan answered 'Then I know nothing about plays'. To which Devine replied, 'You know everything about plays, but you don't know a fucking thing about *Look Back in Anger.*'[30] Rattigan only barely attended the first night. He and Hugh Beaumont wanted to leave at the interval until the critic T. C. Worsley persuaded them to stay.[31]

The support for the English Stage Company's initiative was soon
overwhelming. Osborne's play was acclaimed by the influential
critics Kenneth Tynan and Harold Hobson, and the production was
revived frequently at the Court, soon standing as the banner under
which that disparate band of men (and women), the Angry Young
Men, would assemble. Like many of his contemporaries, Rattigan
decried the new movements, Beckett and Ionesco's turn from
Naturalism, the wild invective of Osborne, the passionate
socialism of Wesker, the increasing influence of Brecht. His
opposition to them was perhaps intemperate, but he knew what
was at stake: 'I may be prejudiced, but I'm pretty sure it won't
survive,' he said in 1960, 'I'm prejudiced because if it *does*
survive, I know I won't.' [32]

Such was the power and influence of the new movement that
Rattigan almost immediately seemed old-fashioned. And
from now on, his plays began to receive an almost automatic
panning. His first play since *Separate Tables* (1954) was *Variation
on a Theme* (1958). But between those dates the critical mood had
changed. To make matters worse, there was the widely publicized
story that nineteen year-old Shelagh Delaney had written the
successful *A Taste of Honey* in two weeks after having seen
Variation on a Theme and deciding that she could do better. A
more sinister aspect of the response was the increasingly open
accusation that Rattigan was dishonestly concealing a covert
homosexual play within an apparently heterosexual one. The two
champions of Osborne's play, Tynan and Hobson, were joined by
Gerard Fay in the *Manchester Guardian* and Alan Brien in the
Spectator to ask 'Are Things What They Seem?' [33]

When he is not being attacked for smuggling furtively homosexual
themes into apparently straight plays, Rattigan is also criticized
for lacking the courage to 'come clean' about his sexuality, both in
his life and in his writing.[34] But neither of these criticisms really
hit the mark. On the one hand, it is rather disingenuous to suggest
that Rattigan should have 'come out'. The 1950s were a difficult
time for homosexual men. The flight to the Soviet Union of
Burgess and Maclean in 1951 sparked off a major witch-hunt
against homosexuals, especially those in prominent positions.
Cecil Beaton and Benjamin Britten were rumoured to be targets.[35]
The police greatly stepped up the investigation and entrapment of
homosexuals and prosecutions rose dramatically at the end of the
forties, reaching a peak in 1953-54. One of their most infamous
arrests for importuning, in October 1953, was that of John
Gielgud.[36]

But neither is it quite correct to imply that somehow Rattigan's
plays are *really* homosexual. This would be to misunderstand the
way that homosexuality figured in the forties and early fifties.
Wartime London saw a considerable expansion in the number of

pubs and bars where homosexual men (and women) could meet. This network sustained a highly sophisticated system of gestural and dress codes, words and phrases that could be used to indicate one's sexual desires, many of them drawn from theatrical slang. But the illegality of any homosexual activity ensured that these codes could never become *too* explicit, *too* clear. Homosexuality, then, was explored and experienced through a series of semi-hidden, semi-open codes of behaviour; the image of the iceberg, with the greater part of its bulk submerged beneath the surface, was frequently employed.[37] And this image is, of course, one of the metaphors often used to describe Rattigan's own playwriting.

Reaction came in the form of a widespread paranoia about the apparent increase in homosexuality. The fifties saw a major drive to seek out, understand, and often 'cure' homosexuality. The impetus of these investigations was to bring the unspeakable and underground activities of, famously, 'Evil Men' into the open, to make it fully visible. The Wolfenden Report of 1957 was, without doubt, a certain kind of liberalizing document in its recommendation that consensual sex between adult men in private be legalized. However the other side of its effect is to reinstate the integrity of those boundaries – private/public, hidden/exposed, homosexual/heterosexual – which homosexuality was broaching. The criticisms of Rattigan are precisely part of this same desire to divide, clarify and expose.

Many of Rattigan's plays were originally written with explicit homosexual characters (*French Without Tears*, *The Deep Blue Sea* and *Separate Tables*, for example), which he then changed.[38] But many more of them hint at homosexual experiences and activities: the relationship between Tony and David in *First Episode*, the Major in *Follow my Leader* who is blackmailed over an incident in Baghdad ('After all,' he explains, 'a chap's only human, and it was a deuced hot night –'),[39] the suspiciously polymorphous servicemen of *While the Sun Shines*, Alexander the Great and T. E. Lawrence from *Adventure Story* and *Ross*, Mr Miller in *The Deep Blue Sea* and several others. Furthermore, rumours of Rattigan's own bachelor life circulated fairly widely. As indicated above, Rattigan always placed great trust in the audiences of his plays, and it was the audience which had to decode and reinterpret these plays. His plays cannot be judged by the criterion of 'honesty' and 'explicitness' that obsessed a generation after Osborne. They are plays which negotiate sexual desire through structures of hint, implications and metaphor. As David Rudkin has suggested, 'the craftsmanship of which we hear so much loose talk seems to me to arise from deep psychological necessity, a drive to organize the energy that arises out of his own pain. Not to batten it down but to invest it with some expressive clarity that speaks immediately to people, yet keeps itself hidden'.[40]

The shifts in the dominant view of both homosexuality and
the theatre that took place in the fifties account for the brutal
decline of Rattigan's career. He continued writing, and while
Ross (1960) was reasonably well received, his ill-judged musical
adaptation of *French Without Tears*, *Joie de Vivre* (1960), was
a complete disaster, not assisted by a liberal bout of laryngitis
among the cast, and the unexpected insanity of the pianist.[41] It
ran for four performances.

During the sixties, Rattigan was himself dogged with ill-health:
pneumonia and hepatitis were followed by leukaemia. When his
death conspicuously failed to transpire, this last diagnosis was
admitted to be incorrect. Despite this, he continued to write,
producing the successful television play *Heart to Heart* in 1962,
and the stage play *Man and Boy* the following year, which
received the same sniping that greeted *Variation on a Theme*. In
1964, he wrote *Nelson – a Portrait in Miniature* for Associated
Television, as part of a short season of his plays.

It was at this point that Rattigan decided to leave Britain and live
abroad. Partly this decision was taken for reasons of health; but
partly Rattigan just seemed no longer to be welcome. Ironically, it
was the same charge being levelled at Rattigan that he had faced
in the thirties, when the newspapers thundered against the those
who had supported the Oxford Union's pacifist motion as 'woolly-
minded Communists, practical jokers and sexual indeterminates'.[42]
As he confessed in an interview late in his life, 'Overnight almost,
we were told we were old-fashioned and effete and corrupt and
finished, and . . . I somehow accepted Tynan's verdict and went
off to Hollywood to write film scripts'.[43] In 1967 he moved to
Bermuda as a tax exile. A stage adaptation of his Nelson play, as
Bequest to the Nation, had a luke-warm reception.

Rattigan had a bad sixties, but his seventies seemed to indicate a
turnaround in his fortunes and reputation. At the end of 1970, a
successful production of *The Winslow Boy* was the first of ten
years of acclaimed revivals. In 1972, Hampstead Theatre revived
While the Sun Shines and a year later the Young Vic was praised
for its *French Without Tears*. In 1976 and 1977 *The Browning
Version* was revived at the King's Head and *Separate Tables* at
the Apollo. Rattigan briefly returned to Britain in 1971, pulled
partly by his renewed fortune and partly by the fact that he was
given a knighthood in the New Year's honours list. Another double
bill followed in 1973: *In Praise of Love* comprised the weak
Before Dawn and the moving tale of emotional concealment and
creativity, *After Lydia*. Critical reception was more respectful than
usual, although the throwaway farce of the first play detracted
from the quality of the second.

Cause Célèbre, commissioned by BBC Radio and others,
concerned the Rattenbury case, in which Alma Rattenbury's aged

husband was beaten to death by her eighteen year-old lover. Shortly after its radio première, Rattigan was diagnosed with bone cancer. Rattigan's response, having been through the false leukaemia scare in the early sixties, was to greet the news with unruffled elegance, welcoming the opportunity to 'work harder and indulge myself more'.[44] The hard work included a play about the Asquith family and a stage adaptation of *Cause Célèbre*, but, as production difficulties began to arise over the latter, the Asquith play slipped out of Rattigan's grasp. Although very ill, he returned to Britain, and on 4 July 1977, he was taken by limousine from his hospital bed to Her Majesty's Theatre, where he watched his last ever première. A fortnight later he had a car drive him around the West End where two of his plays were then running before boarding the plane for the last time. On 30 November 1977, in Bermuda, he died.

As Michael Billington's perceptive obituary noted, 'his whole work is a sustained assault on English middle class values: fear of emotional commitment, terror in the face of passion, apprehension about sex'.[45] In death, Rattigan began once again to be seen as someone critically opposed to the values with which he had so long been associated, a writer dramatizing dark moments of bleak compassion and aching desire.

Notes.

1. Quoted in Rattigan's *Daily Telegraph* obituary (1 December 1977).
2. Michael Darlow and Gillian Hodson. *Terence Rattigan: The Man and His Work*. London and New York: Quartet Books, 1979, p. 26.
3. See, for example, Sheridan Morley. 'Terence Rattigan at 65.' *The Times*. (9 May 1977).
4. Terence Rattigan. Preface. *The Collected Plays of Terence Rattigan: Volume Two*. London: Hamish Hamilton, 1953, p. xv.
5. *Ibid.*, p. viii.
6. *Ibid.*, p. vii.
7. *Ibid.*, p. vii.
8. cf. Sheridan Morley, *op. cit.*
9. Humphrey Carpenter. *OUDS: A Centenary History of the Oxford University Dramatic Society*. With a Prologue by Robert Robinson. Oxford: Oxford University Press, 1985, p. 123.
10. Rattigan may well have reprised this later in life. John Osborne, in his autobiography, recalls a friend showing him a picture of Rattigan performing in an RAF drag show: 'He showed me a photograph of himself with Rattigan, dressed in a *tutu*, carrying a wand, accompanied by a line of aircraftsmen, during which Terry had sung his own show-stopper, 'I'm just about the oldest fairy in the business. I'm quite the oldest fairy that you've ever seen''.' John Osborne. *A Better Class of Person: An Autobiography, Volume I 1929-1956*. London: Faber and Faber, 1981, p. 223.
11. Darlow and Hodson *op. cit.*, p. 83.
12. Norman Gwatkin. Letter to Gilbert Miller, 28 July 1938. in: *Follow My Leader*. Lord Chamberlain's Correspondence: LR 1938. [British Library].
13. Richard Huggett. *Binkie Beaumont: Eminence Grise of the West Theatre 1933-1973*. London: Hodder & Stoughton, 1989, p. 308.

14. Terence Rattigan. Preface. *The Collected Plays of Terence Rattigan: Volume One*. London: Hamish Hamilton, 1953, p. xiv.

15. George Bernard Shaw, in: Keith Newman. *Two Hundred and Fifty Times I Saw a Play: or, Authors, Actors and Audiences*. With the facsimile of a comment by Bernard Shaw. Oxford: Pelagos Press, 1944, p. 2.

16. Henry Channon. *Chips: The Diaries of Sir Henry Channon*. Edited by Robert Rhodes James. Harmondsworth: Penguin, 1974, p. 480. Entry for 29 September 1944.

17. Tom Driberg. *Ruling Passions*. London: Jonathan Cape, 1977, p. 186.

18. See, for example, Norman Hart. 'Introducing Terence Rattigan,' *Theatre World*. xxxi, 171. (April 1939). p. 180 or Ruth Jordan. 'Another Adventure Story,' *Woman's Journal*. (August 1949), pp. 31-32.

19. Audrey Williamson. *Theatre of Two Decades*. New York and London: Macmillan, 1951, p. 100.

20. Terence Rattigan. 'Concerning the Play of Ideas,' *New Statesman and Nation*. (4 March 1950), pp. 241-242.

21. Terence Rattigan. 'The Play of Ideas,' *New Statesman and Nation*. (13 May 1950), pp. 545-546. See also Susan Rusinko, 'Rattigan versus Shaw: The 'Drama of Ideas' Debate'. in: *Shaw: The Annual of Bernard Shaw Studies: Volume Two*. Edited by Stanley Weintraub. University Park, Penn: Pennsylvania State University Press, 1982. pp. 171-78.

22. John Elsom writes that Rattigan's plays 'represented establishment writing'. *Post-War British Drama*. Revised Edition. London: Routledge, 1979, p. 33.

23. B. A. Young. *The Rattigan Version: Sir Terence Rattigan and the Theatre of Character*. Hamish Hamilton: London, 1986, pp. 102-103; and Darlow and Hodson, *op. cit.*, p. 196, 204n.

24. Terence Rattigan. *Coll. Plays: Vol. Two. op. cit.*, pp. xi-xii.

25. *Ibid.*, p. xii.

26. *Ibid.*, p. xiv.

27. *Ibid.*, p. xvi.

28. *Ibid.*, p. xviii.

29. Opened on 17 September 1960. cf. *Plays and Players*. vii, 11 (November 1960).

30. Quoted in Irving Wardle. *The Theatres of George Devine*. London: Jonathan Cape, 1978, p. 180.

31. John Osborne. *Almost a Gentleman: An Autobiography, Volume II 1955-1966*. London: Faber and Faber, 1991, p. 20.

32. Robert Muller. 'Soul-Searching with Terence Rattigan.' *Daily Mail*. (30 April 1960).

33. The headline of Hobson's review in the *Sunday Times*, 11 May 1958.

34. See, for example, Nicholas de Jongh. *Not in Front of the Audience: Homosexuality on Stage*. London: Routledge, 1992, pp. 55-58.

35. Kathleen Tynan. *The Life of Kenneth Tynan*. Corrected Edition. London: Methuen, 1988, p. 118.

36. Cf. Jeffrey Weeks. *Coming Out: Homosexual Politics in Britain from the Nineteenth Century to the Present*. Revised and Updated Edition. London and New York: Quartet, 1990, p. 58; Peter Wildeblood. *Against the Law*. London: Weidenfeld and Nicolson, 1955, p. 46. The story of Gielgud's arrest may be found in Huggett, *op. cit.,* pp. 429-431. It was Gielgud's arrest which apparently inspired Rattigan to write the second part of *Separate Tables*, although again, thanks this time to the Lord Chamberlain, Rattigan had to change the Major's offence to a heterosexual one. See Darlow and Hodson, *op. cit.*, p. 228.

37. See, for example, Rodney Garland's novel about homosexual life in London, *The Heart in Exile*. London: W. H. Allen, 1953, p. 104.

38. See note 36; and also 'Rattigan Talks to John Simon,' *Theatre Arts*. 46 (April 1962), p. 24.

39. Terence Rattigan and Anthony Maurice. *Follow my Leader.* Typescript. Lord Chamberlain Play Collection: 1940/2. Box 2506. [British Library].

40. Quoted in Darlow and Hodson, *op. cit.,* p. 15.

41. B. A. Young, *op. cit.,* p. 162.

42. Quoted in Darlow and Hodson, *op. cit.,* p. 56.

43. Quoted in Sheridan Morley, *op. cit.*

44. Darlow and Hodson, *op. cit.,* p. 308.

45. *Guardian*. (2 December 1977).

After the Dance

By the late 1930s, the Warner Brothers screenwriting contract, into which Rattigan had so reluctantly entered, had become a serious constraint on his life and ambition. *French Without Tears* was firmly resident in the West End; further productions were planned across Europe and America. His income from the run was in excess of £100 per week, but, tied to a seven-year contract, and now saleably prestigious, Rattigan was being hired out by Warner Brothers to other studios. These lucrative deals were always made over his head, while Rattigan continued to draw his £15 weekly wage.

As his fellow-screenwriter, Anthony Powell, recalled, 'one was always aware in Rattigan of a deep inner bitterness, no doubt accentuated by the irksome position in which he found himself at that moment. In the Theatre good publicity such as he was enjoying is something to be taken advantage of without delay'.[1] Rattigan passed his time restlessly, flirting with one of the male executives of the Studio and preparing schoolboyish surprises for his projected successor at the desk.[2] He preferred to spend his time accustoming himself to the wealthy lifestyle of the successful playwright. He moved into a Mayfair apartment, had his suits made by Savile Row tailors, bought a Rolls-Royce, and formed himself into a limited company. But a year after *French Without Tears* had opened, the activity conspicuously missing from his life was writing. With such a huge critical and financial success immediately behind him, Rattigan understandably found the prospect of a new play daunting, and made more so by the time commitment to Warner Brothers.

In September 1937, he was granted leave to attend the New York première of *French Without Tears* (characteristically choosing to stay at the Waldorf Astoria hotel). His boss at Warner Brothers, Irving Asher, followed him out and told him that he had been subcontracted again, this time to Hollywood. Rattigan refused and, despite threats of litigation, won a temporary release from his contract. He threw himself fully into the social gyrations of his Broadway opening and it was there that an idea for a new play began to develop.

French Without Tears was not well received by the American critics; most of them found it engaging but trivial, and many belittled it for 'escapism'. Unusually for him, Rattigan decided to answer this complaint in an article for the *New York Times*. The piece introduces themes that he would later discuss in the 'Play of Ideas' controversy (see pp. x-xi). Entitled 'Drama Without Tears', it defended escapism on the three grounds of 'necessity, preference and tradition'. The first was that given the Lord Chamberlain's antipathy towards contemporary, political subject-matter, even a play which tries deal 'honestly with a topical and controversial subject is likely to be blue-pencilled off the stage'. The second was that for English audiences the crisis in Europe was a more pressing concern than for their American counterparts, and its urgency did not lend itself to measured theatrical prescriptions: 'The war clouds are above their very heads . . . They have not the advantage of such an admirably detached field of vision'.[3] And thirdly, he argues, even more tendentiously, that British drama has tended always to disengage itself from immediate political questions.

Yet Rattigan is careful to insist not that politics is insignificant to playwriting, but that escapism may have its own positive political value. He was an active campaigner against the Franco government in Spain, and his politics at this time were firmly left-wing (he had flirted with Communism). In America, he found himself both attracted and appalled by the New York theatrical high life he was experiencing; and Rattigan may have been encouraged by the American reaction to cast a more critical eye on his social environment than he did in *French Without Tears*. His new play was conceived as a condemnation of the generation before his for its complacency in European politics, which had failed to prevent the drift towards war. Nonetheless, Rattigan's passionate defence of the medium over the message in his *New York Times* article remained unqualified in his preparation for this new play. Hubert Gregg, who was playing Kit Neilan in the New York *French Without Tears*, received an invitation to Rattigan's hotel room. He went rather expecting that he was going to be propositioned but instead found that Rattigan wanted to show him his new play.

But the play, as such, was unwritten; in fact, Rattigan thought so wholly in terms of structure that Gregg was being asked to inspect a skeleton. The manuscript was 'almost diagrammatic . . . There would be a brief stage direction, something like "They sit together on the sofa laughing"; under that a vertical line down the page marked a space labelled "three minutes dialogue"; then there would be another direction, followed by another space for dialogue, all carefully timed'.[4] Unlike *First Episode*, thrown together from a series of undergraduate conversations, or *French Without Tears*, written flat out in a month, *After the Dance* shows the beginning of Rattigan's famous concern for meticulous craft and technique.

The play remained in this form for a while, since in early 1938, Rattigan switched to another project. Given his avowals to the *New York Times*, it is surprising that this new project should have been a political satire. A collaboration with Anthony Goldschmidt, a contemporary at Oxford, *Follow My Leader* was a spoof of the rise of Hitler. It is set in the fictional nation of Moronia, where two leading members of the government and army, Slivovitz and Major Baratsch, are scheming to sabotage each other's reputations and place themselves in power. Reaching a stalemate, they agree to install a puppet figurehead, and choose a plumber, Hans Zedesi, who has turned up to fix the radiator. Zedesi readily takes on this rôle and gives public speeches to massed shouts of 'Up Zedesi!' The play includes satirical parallels with the Reichstag fire, Hitler's seizing of emergency powers, and the Austrian 'elections'. Zedesi meets a young journalist and explains the situation to her; she is arrested, but Zedesi has been stirred and changes a speech at the last minute, abandoning a war with a neighbouring country, dismantling the army, and bringing back the old democratic constitution. Slivovitz and Baratsch flee the country. The humour is broad, and the intention seems to be ridicule rather than articulate protest.

Follow My Leader was scheduled for the autumn of 1938, at the St. James's Theatre, and submitted to the Lord Chamberlain for a licence in July. However, his rules at the time forbade the representation of living people, let alone the satirical mockery of them. At the time Britain was still negotiating with Hitler, and Germany was therefore technically a friendly power, so the Lord Chamberlain consulted the Foreign Office. They replied that they were still 'against this "guying" of the heads of foreign states'.[5] The Lord Chamberlain informed the producers that the play could not be therefore be licensed, and added that he saw little hope of a change in the situation before the end of the year.[6] The disappointment threw Rattigan back on his abandoned New York project.

The play that finally emerged a year later bore little resemblance to *French Without Tears*, which was still packing them in at the Criterion. Rather than try to follow up his proven skill with light comedy, he had written a sombre, reflective piece. With Rattigan's name attached, the producers could easily have cast a number of star names to increase the chance of West End longevity. But Rattigan's agent, A. D. Peters, who put some of his own money into the project, decided to use actors associated with less commercial work. He chose to co-produce with the playwright J. B. Priestley, who had been the director of the innovative Mask Theatre Company, based at the Westminster Theatre, one of the major experimental houses of the 1930s; they brought two actors from the Westminster company into the project, Catherine Lacey and Robert Harris, to play Joan and David Scott-Walker. Both had played in O'Neill, Shaw and Eliot while at the Westminster, and had previously distinguished themselves in a number of Shakespearian rôles. Priestley also brought with him Michael Macowan, who had for three years been a director of the Westminster

Theatre, where he had staged many plays from the modern repertoire, including *Uncle Vanya, The Wild Duck, Heartbreak House* and *Anna Christie*. He had also worked with Lacey and Harris before. For the younger parts, they chose a relative newcomer, the twenty-year-old Anne Firth, and Rattigan's reader from his American hotel room, Hubert Gregg. John was to be played by Martin Walker, an admired comic actor.

In May, *French Without Tears* finally closed, and, only a month later, following a short pre-London tour, *After the Dance* opened at St. James's Theatre. Considerable press excitement preceded the opening night, mostly on the topic of whether Rattigan could repeat the success of his previous play. Given the weight now attached to his new play, Rattigan, always prone to appalling first-night nerves, could hardly bear to watch the opening in London. In fact, he sat in an ante-room to his box, playing chess with his agent, every now and then peeping out to see how it was going.

After the Dance presents us with David and Joan, a married couple in their thirties, who are still trying to live the gaiety of their (and the century's) twenties. Living with them is a parasitical hanger-on from their youth, John. A younger generation is represented by David's cousin, Peter, and his fiancée, Helen. Their outlook is focused on the contemporary political situation, and they see David and Joan's succession of drinking, partying and witty phrase-making as cruelly immoral. David has developed cirrhosis from drinking, and Helen urges him to stop. But during the play, Helen's zeal to reform David turns into love, a love which David unexpectedly returns. When Joan is confronted by their plans to marry, her celebrated stance of affected uncaring makes it impossible to fight against her young pretender, and at the last of her sparkling parties, she throws herself from the balcony. In the final act, David's attempts to reform are foundering, and when John confronts him with the prediction that he will drive Helen, too, to suicide, David writes a letter breaking off his engagement; as he does so, he pours himself another drink, signalling a slow suicide as sure as Joan's.

'This is a different Mr. Rattigan,' declared the headline above the *Daily Express* review. And Rattigan's change of direction was noted approvingly by most of the critics. Anthony Squire in the *News Chronicle* wrote that the story 'is perfect material for the dramatist, provided the dramatist is first-class. Mr. Rattigan has proved beyond a shadow of doubt that he is'. Charles Morgan, writing for the *New York Times*, announced that 'in Mr. Rattigan we have not only a successful writer of farce but a dramatist of serious consequences'. Even James Agate, who had poured scorn on *French Without Tears*, admitted that 'I see nothing here that is not praiseworthy'.

The critics found the characterisation particularly praiseworthy. Ivor Brown in the *Observer* quibbled with aspects of the play but judged that the characters were forcefully drawn: 'his study of Joan, in particular, is first rate'. The *Times* applauded 'the subtlety of Mr. Rattigan's studies of his principal men and women'. Charles Morgan thought the writing of major characters showed 'genuine insight'. The most unreserved praise was for the character of John, and Martin Walker's performance; G. B. Stern in the *Daily Telegraph* found him 'the most attractive character in the play', Ivor Brown admired the way that Walker 'nearly coaxes us into affection for the wretch', and A. E. Wilson in the *Star* called him 'the philosopher of the play'. The audience were in agreement, applauding Walker on every exit.

The reviewer from *Cavalcade* was not alone in predicting that *After the Dance* was 'almost certain to remain on the boards for months to come'. But on 12 August, the play closed, having clocked up only sixty performances. Although some had been highly critical – the *New Statesman* asserted that 'Mr Rattigan has found a fine, fat theme for a comedy, and wasted it upon a melodrama'[7] – the reason for the early closure was most likely the increasing bleakness of the international outlook. Perhaps Rattigan was right when he wrote in the *New York Times* that theatre audiences did not want reminding of political gloom. *After the Dance* is punctuated by references to appeasement and the onrush of war, and the tone becomes increasingly apprehensive as the play enters its third act. Rattigan was always hypersensitive to criticism, and he later dismissed the play as 'turgid' and 'rather heavy', finding its relative failure justified.[8] The play was briefly revived at the Croydon Repertory theatre in February 1940; but it never established itself in the modern repertoire, and, not wanting to spoil his claim of having had 'five solid successes in a row', Rattigan did not include it in his *Collected Plays*.[9] The play was published in 1939, but has never been reprinted until now, and remained unperformed and forgotten for over fifty years.

In the early 1990s, the BBC, under the banner of the 'Performance' season, introduced a series of televised adaptations of stage plays. They laid particular emphasis on reviving British work from the twenty years before *Look Back in Anger* (including productions of Ackland's *Absolute Hell*, Mackenzie's *The Maitlands* and Priestley's *Summer Day's Dream*). In December 1992, under Stuart Burge's direction, they revived *After the Dance,* with Anton Rodgers and Gemma Jones as David and Joan, John Bird as John, and Imogen Stubbs and Richard Lintern as Helen and Peter. The production was highly praised; the *Telegraph* reviewer described Stuart Burge's direction as 'impeccable – understated, with a few minutes of emotional evisceration shocking in their impact. Two hours of joy'.[10] Craig Brown in the *Sunday Times* praised it as 'a subversion of the well-made drama for which Rattigan was later to be dismissed by his juniors'.[11]

After the Dance proved to have aged extremely well. Indeed, the changes in theatrical custom of the past fifty years have largely worked in the play's favour. Certain critics in the late 1930s found the play difficult to take because none of the characters ever attracts our uncomplicated sympathy. Rattigan told journalists that his play was designed as an attack on the Bright Young Things of the 1920s by the next generation. David Scott-Fowler, drinking himself to death and squandering his talent, has echoes of F. Scott Fitzgerald in more than just name. But as most critics have remarked, the play itself did not come out that way. Some critics of the first production felt that in fact 'the older generation have Mr. Rattigan's vote' (*Times*); but as Rattigan's Oxford contemporary, Paul Dehn, writing in the *Sunday Chronicle*, reminds us, even then, the play divided its audience by age. In fact, as *After the Dance* appears now, it endorses neither old nor young, and instead plays with our sympathies to add layer upon layer of complexity to our identification, building to an ending which defies simple emotional categorisation.

The first act begins with the generational battle lines fairly clearly drawn. Peter and John both nurse hangovers, but while John luxuriates in his, delighting in his 'parasitical' lifestyle, Peter bashes earnestly at his typewriter, deriding John's lack of social commitment. These two camps are soon joined by Joan and Helen. Helen and Peter mockingly discuss the louche frivolity of the old, while Rattigan has given Joan a register which seems cruelly inadequate for all situations but drinking and gossip. She describes the serious political intentions of the young as 'nice' (p. 8), seems aghast at all suggestions that she is not still twenty-one, and uses the vogue word 'torture' to describe subjects as diverse as Julia's new toy-boy, modern music and King Bomba of Naples.

A more straightforward satirical portrait of the grimmer members of the Bright Young Things is given in the character of Julia. She explodes into the flat, forgets to introduce her boyfriend (and then cannot remember his name), and lets fly with a string of ever more alarmingly violent anecdotes from the hilarious social life of her circle. (Noël Coward's New York revue from the same year, *Set to Music*, included the song 'I Went to a Marvellous Party', which satirised such glittering excesses in similar vein. But Coward was always more inclined to sympathise with the Bright Young generation, never satirising them with the scorn that *After the Dance* does, and indeed is arguably part of the very generation Rattigan is attacking.)

However, even at the start, this picture is not so simple. The sheer absurdity of Julia leaves the way clear for a more complex portrait of Joan and David. For the first ten minutes of the play, David is off-stage, and his image is built up as a ragingly drunken, lethally hungover mess of a man. But when he makes his first appearance, we are startled by a man who appears entirely *compos mentis*, and who smartly chides Peter for a simple error in his historical know-ledge. And when Helen's brother, George, tries to join in the plot to let David be medically examined, he sees right through the clichéd jocularity of his bedside manner (p. 19). On Joan's side, we occasionally notice that her flippancy can seem a little forced. When Helen tells her that she has arranged for her brother to examine David, Joan replies that David 'thinks all doctors are liars and thieves and bores. (*As an afterthought.*) So they are, of course' (p. 11).

Conversely, the younger characters are shown to be rather priggish in their youthful zeal. Like Irina in Chekhov's *Three Sisters,* they talk piously about the character-building qualities of hard work: 'They might all have been quite different if they'd been given a proper chance. It must be awful having to grow up without having to work' (p. 17). This comment is neatly challenged, both by the obvious fact that Peter gains very little value from the 'hard work' he is doing, and later by Miss Potter's forthright attitude:

JOHN. You haven't any objection to not working?

MISS POTTER. Who has?

JOHN. Your predecessor had.

MISS POTTER. Then she was a fool. (p. 64)

Rattigan allows for a complex series of motifs to underpin the first act, reinforcing the problem that Helen identifies: the fast lifestyle of the first generation to enjoy their youth after the 1914-18 War had the value of a gesture, but it is 'a gesture that hasn't any meaning now – so you should stop making it' (p. 28). This idea is picked up when Joan, who dislikes modern tunes, puts on a record from her youth; but the scratched old record jumps, and would repeat itself indefinitely if Helen didn't lift the needle. This simple image prefigures the salvation she plans for David.

The empty repetition of gestures from David and Joan's youth is also pointed up through their concerns for the forms of speech and behaviour, rather than the content. John makes a rather cruel retort to Joan, but only criticises himself for his failure of wit (p. 8); Joan enters the room in the middle of a row between David and John, and asks, 'Are you two having what are popularly known as words?' (p. 37), and when Helen moves to strike the glass of whisky from his hand for a second time, he comments: 'that little gesture . . . was effective the first time, but it might lose its point if you do it again' (p. 27). Tellingly, David is a historian, but one concerned with a marginal, forgotten figure from the past.

The relationships begin to shift, and Rattigan's choreography of the end of Act One is impressively economical in the way this shift is plotted. Helen has implored David to give up his drinking and Joan and David acknowledge privately that Helen loves him. After she leaves, everyone gets ready for lunch, Joan fixing the drinks; but the dialogue is entirely given over to a conversation between Joan and John. David is curiously silent, but we soon get a hint unread by anyone else on stage of the direction of his thoughts, as he wanders in to the dining room. John goes to the gramophone to turn the music up, and calls out that David has forgotten to take in his whisky. And with this suggestion that David is shifting his affections towards Helen, the record begins to repeat itself again as the lights fade.

In the second act, Rattigan draws together many of his threads to show Joan's decline. It soon becomes clear that Joan's enforced joviality had led her into a situation she has not the resources to escape. A foretaste is given early in the scene, when Joan gaily announces the need for more glasses at the party; but when Helen unexpectedly appears to talk to David, Joan is unsettled by this turn of events, but cannot let her personal fears appear to outweigh her party plans, and is forced to leave them alone together. The only hint is in her awkward response to Helen:

> HELEN. . . . You see, it's David I really want to see.
>
> JOAN. Oh! (*Fatuously.*) Well, he's here all right, aren't you, David. (p. 39)

And on Joan's return, we watch Helen, abrim with zealous innocence, inform her that she and David wish to get married. When she repeats to Joan what David believes, that neither he nor Joan have ever loved each other, Joan is forced to go along with this story. Her flippant rhetoric has trapped her into finding it impossible to admit her real feelings (to do so would, presumably, be 'boring'). Helen's unintentional cruelty amplifies the scene's tension: she tries to be sympathetic, drawing out Joan's genuine misery. But Joan cannot allow this and is forced to lighten the situation even further, telling half-hearted anecdotes about their wedding, and joking, 'Let's have a quiet little divorce, shall we, with only the family as guests' (p. 49). It is the audience that supplies what is going on 'under the surface', guided by tiny hints like Joan's brokenly distracted response to Helen's concern:

> HELEN. Thank you, Joan, for taking this so well.
>
> JOAN. Have I taken it well? I didn't know. (p. 50)

We are awaiting the moment when Joan will be left alone to show her grief. And teasingly, as Joan is genteelly showing Helen out, Rattigan delays this moment fractionally as the front door sticks. This tiny moment builds the tension even further so that when Joan finally breaks down in front of John, the moment is devastating. She turns from the mirror and we see the full, ugly embarrassment of her misery. The woman who has hidden her desires behind gaiety and unconcern is now moved to the shockingly complete admission: 'Oh, John, I need him so much – so much more than Helen' (p. 51).

But even in this compelling scene the play does not let us simply wallow in sympathy. We are not allowed to forget that, Joan's feelings aside, David might well be happier with Helen. At the end of the scene, David does not know that Helen has told Joan about their plans. Joan cannot admit to her real feelings, except as displaced onto David's manuscript, found lying in the wastepaper basket where Helen had thrown it. It is moving to hear Joan plead with him to hold onto the manuscript, 'as a sentimental memory, if nothing else' (p. 52), when we can guess that she is talking about her own marriage. But against this we also hear the inadequacy of her attempts, on a more literal level, to encourage him with the book he has so brusquely dismissed: 'Are you sure you're right? I think it's very good' (p. 52). We know that the book probably is as bad as Helen has described it. While we feel for Joan, we are also aware that she has already been made redundant by Helen's ruthless honesty.

It has become a commonplace to criticise Rattigan's plays on the grounds that they repressedly avoid the display of emotion. But in fact the reverse is true. What is remarkable in this play is the skill with which Rattigan depicts the appalling forces that conspire to make emotions impossible to express, *and* the emotions which lie undeclared. Although the characters do not easily admit their feelings to each other on stage, Rattigan gives us enough information to chart the violence meted out by one generation on the other, and to endow the tiniest moments with a fierce intensity.

Nowhere is this better shown than in the party scene, the centrepiece of *After the Dance*. As Joan wanders around the party, playing the perfect hostess in the perfect dress, with each person she meets her state of mind becomes more and more explicit; *but nowhere in the scene does she ever articulate her feelings.* Rattigan builds up the depths behind her carefree façade by hint, indirection and irony. As the scene opens, everyone, to Joan's discomfort, is exchanging snippets of gossip. There is a cruel double-take as Moya begins, 'Joan, isn't it terrible? It's not true,' before ending, 'about Doris and the taximan' (p. 54). Joan's discomfort at being on the other end of her own habitual gossip is a step on the way to her suicide, at which point she becomes another figure in the tragic trail of hilarious party tales that Julia and Moya trade. By the beginning of Act Three, Helen is dismissing Joan's death as an accident, just as Julia did with a similar story in Act One. As the play progresses, we hear more and more darkly the unconsciously violent language of their set's slang in which things they don't like are dubbed 'torture', things they do as 'agony', where a piece of music can be praised because 'it tears me to shreds' (p. 25), and Joan can announce of a thrilling new piece of scandal 'I just can't wait to tell Moya. It'll kill her' (p. 58).

In Joan's brief conversation with David, his confession that he found it hard to know when or how he fell in love with Helen, and that he thought it would have been boring to mention his cirrhosis, is charged with irony, since he is articulating the feelings that Joan cannot. We can hear in these words the unspoken image of Joan's love for her husband and her belief that it would have bored him to admit it. In the BBC production, Gemma Jones only let Anton Rodgers's David glimpse the pain underlying Joan's vivacity once: David hears the sounds from next door and offers to bring the guests in, and Jones grabbed clumsily at him, her 'No, don't go' filled with a brief, awkward panic.

Through the play of these hints and ironies, Rattigan gives us a moving critique of these characters, rather than, as is often said, a simple endorsement of them; the disparaging tag of 'french window playwright' is silently countered here by the fact that these french windows open onto nothing but a fifty foot drop. And the image at the end of the central act, the empty balcony, is emblematic of Rattigan's technique; it is a double negative: nothing, which nobody sees. And yet the structure in which Rattigan has placed this emptiness allows us to fill this void with a complete picture of Joan's fall.

In 1939, some of the critics of *After the Dance* felt that after the death of the most sympathetic character, Joan, there was nowhere for the play to go. But to have let it end at Joan's suicide would have been sentimental. It is to Rattigan's credit that he remorselessly shows us the lives of his characters after the party is over. The events have moved on six months, and this leap allows us to see precisely how little Joan's death has affected these characters. In fact, it is now little more than another occasion for gossip, or for absurd over-theatrical demonstration of Julia Browne's hypersensitivity; turning up to invite David to another party at Moya's, she announces, 'I've got to admit I hate coming to this flat at all. It gives me the shudders every time I look at that balcony'. (Over)emphasising her point, she approaches the balcony, looks at it and turns with a shudder (p. 77). Helen seems to have hardened to the death; when Miss Potter presses her for information, Helen replies coolly that she left before it happened, thus erasing any sense of responsibility for Joan's suicide.

The third act builds to John's confrontation with David. Rattigan gives us little information about David's feelings, except to show him asking Helen not to mention Joan ('You still can't bear me to talk about Joan, can you?' p. 69), invoking our conventional

sympathy towards the grieving. We indulge him as he slips back
into old habits, planning evenings at Moya's party and organising
to eat out, although we can plainly see that his book on Talleyrand
will be a long time coming. John refuses to let David (and us)
overindulge himself in grief, perceiving that this display of feeling
is just a way of not facing his own complicity in Joan's death.

John's own development through the play opens the last act; rather
than just present the developing relationship between David and
Helen, it becomes a dialogue between these events and the wider
political scene. As the play opens, John comfortably identifies as a
parasite; but throughout the play it becomes clear that his entire
lack of responsibility has given him a valuable freedom. He is the
person who continually irritated Joan by gaily reminding her that
their generation is no longer young; and at the party, Rattigan
neatly uses John to undermine the easier kinds of objections to the
aging flappers' lifestyle:

> ARTHUR. . . . The next war wouldn't be there if people took
> the trouble to prevent it.
>
> JOHN. I hope people do prevent it. I shall be very grateful to
> them.
>
> ARTHUR. We had our chance to do it after the last war, but we
> all ran away instead. The awful thing is that we're still
> running away. I didn't realise that so much until tonight.
>
> JOHN. You're not running away, Arthur. You're cleaning
> windows.
>
> ARTHUR. Yes, I'm cleaning windows.
>
> JOHN. I'm sure you have to face life squarely to clean
> windows for a living.
>
> ARTHUR *is silent.* (p. 56)

Lying on the sofa for most of the play, John keeps up a witty
stream of sardonic remarks on the idealistic and self-deluding
arrogance of the other characters. Although he has accepted the
offer of a job in Arthur's window-cleaning firm, he is stealing
several of John's clothes and plans to be drunk before the train
pulls into Manchester; his new-found seriousness is obviously
skin-deep. In the third act, we become aware that David's failure
to reform himself may well destroy Helen, that Peter has used an
unspoken emotional blackmail to extract money out of David, and
that Helen's idealistic dream of an ascetic rural life free of running
water and electricity will be deeply unsuitable for David. John's
parasitism seems more than matched by that of his earnest friends.

But the approach of war is making itself felt. Even Julia is affected when her young boyfriend is conscripted; more chilling is the way Peter's earlier hopes have hollowed into a grim pessimism, as he laughs at the very idea that he might have a future (p. 75). For these people, as Rattigan wrote in the *New York Times*, the war clouds are above their very heads. In the final moments of the play, as David sits down to write his letter ending his relationship with Helen, our feelings are divided. John may be right in advising David to leave Helen, but, as David reaches for the whisky decanter, we know that this is a suicide as certain as Joan's from the balcony. In the last summer before the Second World War, this image would have reverberated hollowly with the slide into war. Our sympathies are caught between John's clear-sighted acknowledgement of David's limitations, and the pessimistic implication of this for the wider situation.

In early July, plans were afoot to stage an adaptation of *A Tale of Two Cities* by Rattigan and John Gielgud, and Rattigan was engaged in translating two comedies from French and Italian. But the outbreak of war put paid to the former, and the early closure of *After the Dance* dented Rattigan's morale, and he abandoned the translations too. Another application to license a re-written *Follow My Leader* was refused in July 1939, especially after the German Embassy advised that it would not be 'helpful in improving Anglo-German relations'.[12] (Evidently the fact that Von Ribbentrop, the German ambassador, had apparently been to see *French Without Tears* several times, approving its depiction of English effeteness and disrespect for the armed forces, held no sway.) Another plan to stage it in a club theatre came to nothing. Once war had been declared a licence could be given, but by the time that *Follow My Leader* reached the stage at the beginning of 1940, the play's jovial derision was ill-matched to the national crisis, and its run barely exceeded two weeks.

Rattigan never lost his belief that popular success was the key to personal fulfilment, and these failures cast him into a deep depression which rendered him unable to write. Under the advice of his psychiatrist, the pacifist Rattigan applied to join the Air Force. From these experiences, he would both lose his writer's block and find the material for his next two plays, *Flare Path* and *While the Sun Shines*. Meanwhile, *After the Dance* lay forgotten; he would recapture its power and sophistication in later plays, but the play now stands to us as one of his most unhesitatingly serious and complex pieces, a shattering picture of emotional violence.

DAN REBELLATO

Notes

1. Anthony Powell. *To Keep the Ball Rolling – Memoirs Volume Three: Faces in My Time.* London: Heinemann, 1980, p. 40.

2. Michael Darlow and Gillian Hodson. *Terence Rattigan: The Man and His Work.* London and New York: Quartet Books, 1979, p. 75-76.

3. Terence Rattigan. 'Drama Without Tears,' *New York Times.* Section XI. (10 October 1937), p. 3.

4. Hubert Gregg, quoted in B. A. Young. *The Rattigan Version: Sir Terence Rattigan and the Theatre of Character.* Hamish Hamilton: London, 1986, p. 33.

5. Memo. Undated [c.26 July 1938]. *Follow My Leader*, in: Lord Chamberlain's Correspondence: LR 1938. [British Library].

6. Norman Gwatkin. Letter to Gilbert Miller, 28 July 1938. Ibid.

7. Reviews quoted from the Production File for *After the Dance*. St James's Theatre, 21 June 1939, in the Theatre Museum, London.

8. Philip Oakes. 'Comédie Anglaise.' Radio Times. (13 May 1976), p. 64.

9. Preface to *The Collected Plays of Terence Rattigan*: Volume One. London: Hamish Hamilton, 1953, p. ix.

10. *Telegraph*, (5 December 1992).

11. *Sunday Times*, (6 December 1992).

12. Letter from German Embassy to Lord Chamberlain, 3 August 1939. *Follow My Leader*. Lord Chamberlain's Correspondence, op. cit.

Notes.

1. Anthony Powell. *To Keep the Ball Rolling – Memoirs Volume Three: Faces in My Time.* London: Heinemann, 1980, p. 40.

2. Michael Darlow and Gillian Hodson. *Terence Rattigan: The Man and His Work.* London and New York: Quartet Books, 1979, p. 75-76.

3. Terence Rattigan. 'Drama Without Tears,' *New York Times.* Section XI. (10 October 1937), p. 3.

4. Hubert Gregg, quoted in B. A. Young. *The Rattigan Version: Sir Terence Rattigan and the Theatre of Character.* Hamish Hamilton: London, 1986, p. 33.

5. Memo. Undated [c.26 July 1938]. *Follow My Leader*, in: Lord Chamberlain's Correspondence: LR 1938. [British Library].

6. Norman Gwatkin. Letter to Gilbert Miller, 28 July 1938. Ibid.

7. Reviews quoted from the Production File for *After the Dance*. St James's Theatre, 21 June 1939, in the Theatre Museum, London.

8. Philip Oakes. 'Comédie Anglaise.' Radio Times. (13 May 1976), p. 64.

9. Preface to *The Collected Plays of Terence Rattigan*: Volume One. London: Hamish Hamilton, 1953, p. ix.

10. *Telegraph*, (5 December 1992).

11. *Sunday Times*, (6 December 1992).

12. Letter from German Embassy to Lord Chamberlain, 3 August 1939. *Follow My Leader*. Lord Chamberlain's Correspondence, op. cit.

13. Reviews published in *Theatre Record*, xxii, 21 (15 October 2002), pp. 1376-1377.

14. Reviews published in *Theatre Record*, xxx, 12 (6 July 2010), pp. 638-642.

Publisher's note

In preparing this revised edition, it was noticed that Rattigan's text gives the interval between Acts Two and Three variously as three and six months. We have standardised this to six months, which accords with the 2010 National Theatre revival.

List of Rattigan's Produced Plays

Title	British Première	New York Première
First Episode (with Philip Heimann)	'Q' Theatre, Surrey, 11 Sept 1933, trans. Comedy Th, 26 January 1934	Ritz Theatre 17 September 1934
French Without Tears	Criterion Th, 6 Nov 1936	Henry Miller Th, 28 Sept 1937
After the Dance	St James's Th, 21 June 1939	
Follow My Leader (with Anthony Maurice, alias Tony Goldschmidt)	Apollo Th, 16 Jan 1940	
Grey Farm (with Hector Bolitho)		Hudson Th, 3 May 1940
Flare Path	Apollo Th, 13 Aug 1942	Henry Miller Th, 23 Dec 1942
While the Sun Shines	Globe Th, 24 Dec 1943	Lyceum Th, 19 Sept 1944
Love in Idleness	Lyric Th, 20 Dec 1944	Empire Th (as *O Mistress Mine*), 23 Jan 1946
The Winslow Boy	Lyric Th, 23 May 1946	Empire Th, 29 October 1947
Playbill (The Browning Version, Harlequinade)	Phoenix Th, 8 Sept 1948	Coronet Th, 12 October 1949
Adventure Story	St James's Th, 17 March 1949	
A Tale of Two Cities (adapt from Dickens, with John Gielgud)	St Brendan's College Dramatic Scy, Clifton, 23 Jan 1950	
Who is Sylvia?	Criterion Th, 24 Oct 1950	
Final Test (tv)	BBC TV 29 July 1951	

The Deep Blue Sea	Duchess Th, 6 March 1952	Morosco Th, 5 Nov 1952
The Sleeping Prince	Phoenix Th, 5 November 1953	Coronet Th, 1 November 1956
Separate Tables (*Table by the Window, Table Number Seven*)	St James's Th, 22 Sept 1954	Music Box Th, 25 Oct 1956
Variation on a Theme	Globe Th, 8 May 1958	
Ross	Theatre Royal, Haymarket, 12 May 1960	Eugene O'Neill Th, 26 Dec 1961
Joie de Vivre (with Robert Stolz, Paul Dehn)	Queen's Th, 14 July 1960	
Heart to Heart (tv)	BBC TV, 6 Dec 1962	
Man and Boy	Queen's Th, 4 Sept 1963	Brooks Atkinson Th, 12 Nov 1963
Ninety Years On (tv)	BBC TV, 29 Nov 1964	
Nelson – a Portrait in Miniature (tv)	Associated Television, 21 March 1966	
All on Her Own (tv) [adapted for stage as *Duologue*]	BBC 2, 25 Sept 1968 King's Head, Feb 1976	
A Bequest to the Nation	Theatre Royal, Haymarket, 23 Sept 1970	
High Summer (tv)	Thames TV, 12 Sept 1972	
In Praise of Love (*After Lydia, Before Dawn*)	Duchess Th, 27 Sept 1973	Morosco Th, 10 Dec 1974
Cause Célèbre (radio)	BBC Radio 4 27 Oct 1975	
Cause Célèbre (stage)	Her Majesty's Th, 4 July 1977	

AFTER THE DANCE

7m 6f + Guests (handwritten)

Characters

M JOHN REID ~~38~~ (mid 30s – early 40s) (handwritten)
M PETER SCOTT-FOWLER (21) (handwritten)
F WILLIAMS (~~40s~~ any age) (handwritten)
F JOAN SCOTT-FOWLER (~~38~~ mid 30s – early 40s) (handwritten)
F HELEN BANNER (20) (handwritten)
M DR GEORGE BANNER (25) (handwritten)
F JULIA BROWNE (30s – 40s) (handwritten)
M CYRIL CARTER (20s) (handwritten)
M DAVID SCOTT-FOWLER (38) (handwritten)
F MOYA LEXINGTON (30s – 40s) (handwritten)
M LAWRENCE WALTERS (any age) (handwritten)
M ARTHUR POWER (30s – 40s) (handwritten)
F MISS POTTER (40s) (handwritten)
GUESTS

Act One	A morning in August.
Act Two, Scene One	A week later, afternoon.
Act Two, Scene Two	The same night.
Act Three	Six months later, late afternoon.

*The action takes place in the drawing-room of the Scott-Fowlers'
flat in Mayfair.*

After the Dance was first produced at the St James's Theatre,
London on 21 June 1939, with the following cast:

JOHN REID	Martin Walker
PETER SCOTT-FOWLER	Hubert Gregg
WILLIAMS	Gordon Court
JOAN SCOTT-FOWLER	Catherine Lacey
HELEN BANNER	Anne Firth
DR GEORGE BANNER	Robert Kempson
JULIA BROWNE	Viola Lyel
CYRIL CARTER	Leonard Coppins
DAVID SCOTT-FOWLER	Robert Harris
MOYA LEXINGTON	Millicent Wolf
LAWRENCE WALTERS	Osmund Willson
ARTHUR POWER	Henry Caine
MISS POTTER	Lois Heatherley

The play was produced by Michael Macowan

Act One

Scene. The drawing-room of the SCOTT-FOWLERS' *top-floor flat in Mayfair. It is a large room, furnished rather in the manner of the early nineteen twenties, but not exaggeratedly so. There is a piano upstage left. A door downstage left leads into* DAVID's *bedroom. Another door upstage left leads to the hall and the rest of the flat. This door, when opened, affords a view of the hall, front door, and* JOAN's *bedroom door. At the back, large french windows lead on to a small rectangular balcony and give a view of treetops in Hyde Park, and beyond the roofs of distant buildings.*

At the rise of the curtain: JOHN REID, *fat, red-faced, about thirty-seven, is lying on his back on the sofa, dressed in pyjamas and dressing-gown. A copy of* The Times *drapes his stomach. He has evidently fallen asleep while reading. A young man of about twenty-one,* PETER SCOTT-FOWLER, *is busy typing at a table with his back to* JOHN. WILLIAMS, *the butler, comes through the door and crosses the stage to the door of* DAVID's *bedroom with a tray on which is a glass of orange juice and a coffee pot. He knocks and goes in.* PETER *glances at the clock above his head. The hands stand at twelve-thirty.*

PETER. David's alive, anyhow, which is something. (*He continues to type. After three or four words he stops.*) How do you spell Wittelsbach, John?

There is no answer. PETER *turns round in his chair, sees* JOHN *is asleep, and shakes his head wearily. He continues with his work.* WILLIAMS *comes out of* DAVID's *room and goes over to the sofa, where he stands looking down at* JOHN. *He coughs gently. That having had no effect, he shakes him.* JOHN *opens his eyes without moving.*

WILLIAMS. Excuse me sir, but Mr Scott-Fowler wants to know if you can let him have your bottle of bicarbonate of soda. He seems to have run out of his.

JOHN. It's on my table by my bed.

WILLIAMS. Thank you, sir.

WILLIAMS *goes out.*

JOHN. What was I saying?

PETER. You weren't saying anything. You were in a drunken coma.

JOHN. I haven't had a drink yet.

PETER. No, but I bet you've a bit of a hangover.

JOHN. On the contrary, I feel extremely well this morning.

PETER. (*Turning round.*) Haven't you really got a hangover? Honestly?

JOHN. Honestly.

PETER. There's no justice in life. I must have drunk an eighth of what you and David and the rest of you drank last night, and I've got a head that's apt to explode any minute. How do you do it?

JOHN. It's simply a matter of faith.

PETER. And bicarbonate of soda.

JOHN. (*Drowsily.*) That helps. (*He closes his eyes.*)

PETER. Hey, before you go to sleep again tell me how to spell Wittelsbach.

JOHN. Does is matter?

PETER. Yes, it does.

JOHN. (*With an effort.*) W-I-T-T-E-L-S-B-A-C-H.

PETER. Thanks.

JOHN. What are you doing? Writing David's book for him?

PETER. I'm typing out the stuff he dictated last night. And I want to get it finished this morning, so kindly go to sleep again and don't interrupt.

JOHN. Last night? Did you say he dictated to you last night?

PETER. Well, this morning, to be exact. From two till five.

JOHN. But when I went to bed he was as drunk as I was.

PETER. The stuff he dictated seemed to make sense all right.

JOHN. It's cruelty to children. Isn't there some secretaries' union or something you could complain to?

PETER. Oh, I don't mind. After two weeks of sitting about doing nothing, it was quite a relief to have some work to do at last.

JOHN. Eager little thing, aren't you?

PETER. (*Hotly.*) I hate wasting my time, if that's what you mean. And I hate taking five pounds a week for doing nothing.

JOHN. Why?

PETER. Because I believe one ought to work for one's living.

JOHN. (*Stretching himself.*) It's an interesting article of faith. I don't remember having heard it before.

PETER. No, I don't suppose you have.

JOHN. But if you're in the happy position of being able to live without working, which you are, what are you fussing about?

PETER. I'm fussing about being a poor relation taking charity from my rich cousin.

JOHN. I can understand you fussing about being a poor relation, but not about taking charity from your rich cousin.

PETER. Oh, it's no good talking to you. You wouldn't understand what I felt about it in a month of Sundays.

He starts to type again. JOHN *gets up, stretches himself, and goes to a table on which is arrayed an army of bottles. He starts to pour himself out a drink.*

PETER. I wish to God you'd shut up and leave me to do this stuff in peace.

JOHN. What's the hurry?

WILLIAMS *comes in with a bottle of bicarbonate of soda on a tray.*

PETER. If I don't finish typing it by lunch time, David will kick up hell.

WILLIAMS *knocks at the door of* DAVID*'s room and goes in.*

JOHN. I don't think you need worry. I should think it's extremely unlikely that David remembers that he dictated to you at all last night, much less what he dictated.

PETER. Go to sleep, there's a nice fellow.

JOHN. (*Settling himself comfortably in the cushions.*) Now, here are you and I, neither of us a member of the moneyed classes, yet both possessing the advantage of being able to live as a parasite on one of them. You by means of a blood relationship, I by means of a certain ability to act as a kind of court jester. Here we are, nicely installed in a rich man's flat, enjoying all the luxuries of life at his expense –

WILLIAMS *comes out of* DAVID*'s room.*

WILLIAMS. (*To* PETER.) Mr Scott-Fowler says would you let him see the stuff he dictated last night.

PETER. (*Flustered.*) Oh! Would you tell him that I'm afraid I haven't quite finished it all. Tell him I'll finish the rest by lunch time, if only Mr Reid would stop talking for a second.

WILLIAMS. Yes, sir.

PETER. And give him this. It's what I've done up to now.

WILLIAMS. Yes, sir.

WILLIAMS goes back into DAVID's *room.*

PETER. There, you see. What did I tell you?

JOHN. I'm contrite. I shan't disturb you again.

He takes up The Times. PETER *continues typing.* WILLIAMS *comes out of* DAVID's *room.*

WILLIAMS. (*To* PETER.) Mr Scott-Fowler says you needn't bother to finish the rest of it until he's read what you've done, sir.

PETER. Oh, thanks.

With a vaguely disappointed air, he starts to put away the typewriter.

WILLIAMS *goes out.* JOHN *lays down* The Times.

JOHN. Now, as I say, we are both in the fortunate position of being able to live as parasites on David –

PETER. Oh, shut up. You may not be interrupting me now, but you still bore me.

JOHN. You don't like being told you're a parasite?

PETER. No, I don't.

JOHN *chuckles gently.*

What are you laughing at?

JOHN. I'm laughing at the thought of you, all young and fresh and eager, coming down from Oxford with the idea of making your own way in the world, of starting at the bottom of something and working your way to the top – I'm using your language – and what happens to you? You can't find a job, because they're all filled mostly by people who started at the top of something and worked their way to the bottom.

PETER. (*Quite angry.*) That's a typical John Reid remark, if ever there was one. It's not original, it doesn't mean a thing, and it's not funny.

JOHN. (*Sleepily.*) Have I annoyed you, my little man?

PETER. Certainly not. Nothing you could say could possibly annoy me.

JOHN *smiles with closed eyes.*

JOHN. (*After a slight pause.*) Supposing you got a ten-pound-a-week job tomorrow, what would be the first thing you would do?

PETER *picks up a paper and makes a pretence of reading.*

JOHN *holds up his hand.*

JOHN. Don't tell me. I know. You'd marry that girl friend of yours, Helen What's-her-name. You'd settle down in a little two-room flat in Balham or somewhere, with a delicious view of the gas works and the dinkiest little kitchenette you ever saw. Every morning at eight you'll get up and jump into a refreshing cold tub – (*He puts his hand up to his mouth as if a sudden wave of nausea had hit him.*) I shouldn't have said that. (*He lies still for a moment with closed eyes. When he goes on his voice is very drowsy.*) Time marches drearily on, and they give you a rise to twelve pounds ten a week. So you start to have babies, a roomful of hideous, squalling, messy babies – babies – everywhere – in the living-room – on the bed – under the bed – in the kitchenette – (*His voice has been getting gradually more indistinct. It now fades to a slight grunt and silence.* PETER *throws away his paper and goes over to the sofa, where he stands looking down at* JOHN*'s sleeping face, which now wears an angelic smile.*)

JOAN SCOTT-FOWLER *comes out of her room in pyjamas and dressing-gown. She is in the early thirties, with looks that once were good, but have faded more than they should, considering her age. This is accentuated at the moment by the fact that she has just got out of bed without troubling to do much about her appearance.*

JOAN. (*With her hand to her head.*) Bring me the pledge. I want to sign it.

PETER. Hello, Joan. How do you feel?

JOAN. I'm not sure yet. (*She sees* JOHN*, and goes over to the sofa. In* JOHN*'s ear loudly.*) Boo!

JOHN. (*Opening his eyes.*) Good morning, Joan. You look awful.

JOAN. No beauty yourself, darling, in this gay morning light. I see you've been at the gin.

JOHN. There's plenty left.

JOAN. Get me some, my pet, would you?

JOHN. (*Without moving.*) Get it yourself, angel.

PETER *goes to the drink table.*

PETER. Tonic, or soda?

JOAN. Oh, thanks so much, Peter darling. Tonic, please, right up.

JOHN. I forgot there was a gentleman in the room.

JOAN. (*To* JOHN.) You're an infuriating man. I can't think why David and I put up with you.

JOHN. I can't think why I put up with you. (*He looks round, ashamed of himself.*) That wasn't too good, was it?

JOAN. No, it wasn't.

PETER *brings her over the drink.*

Thanks so much. You're an angel. (*She looks up at him.*) My God! Come here, Peter, let me look at you.

JOAN *gazes into his face earnestly.*

It's wonderful. How do you do it?

PETER. Do what?

JOAN. How do you manage to look like that after staying up till five?

PETER. I don't stay up till five very often. I suppose that's why. (*He wanders away.*)

JOHN. Our little Peter is in one of those moods this morning when he thinks we're all wasters, rotters, outsiders, cads and white trash.

JOAN. You don't, do you Peter?

PETER. I certainly never said so.

JOAN. That wasn't a very gracious denial, I must say.

JOHN. Don't blame him too much. I've been telling him it's the fault of his generation.

JOAN. There's nothing wrong with his generation. They're just serious-minded, that's all. I think it's very nice.

JOHN. You don't think anything of the sort. You think they're bores, and so do I. Whatever people may have said about us when we were young, they could never have said we were bores.

JOAN. What do you mean, 'When we were young'?

JOHN. We were once, darling, a long time ago. Don't you remember?

JOAN. I hate you this morning, John. Why don't you go back to bed and sleep it off?

JOHN. I think perhaps that's quite a good idea. (*He gets up and stretches himself.*) What's for lunch?

JOAN. Let me see. A stew of some sort, I think.

JOHN. Using up that old hen we had last night for dinner, I suppose. Why I stay in this house I don't know. (*He goes out left.*)

JOAN. Are you in for lunch, Peter?

PETER. No, I'm taking Helen out. I should have told you. I'm sorry.

JOAN. That's quite all right. Is Helen coming round here?

PETER. Yes, about one. Do you mind?

JOAN. Really, darling, why on earth should I mind?

PETER. I don't know. I just thought it might be taking things a bit for granted, inviting people round here without asking you or David.

JOAN. But I adore Helen. I think she's an angel. Besides she's round here so often these days she's almost one of the family. I suppose you'll be getting married to her soon.

PETER. (*Abruptly.*) As soon as we possibly can.

JOAN. What's the hurry?

PETER. I'm very much in love with her.

JOAN. Then what have you got to worry about? You're in love with Helen and Helen's in love with you.

PETER. It's only that I'm frightened from one day to the next that she won't go on being in love with me.

JOAN. How much would you mind if she didn't?

PETER. I don't like to think about it much.

JOAN. Well, after all, you were at Oxford with her, so that must be two years you've been together.

PETER. Been together?

JOAN. Peter, don't tell me you are still a couple of dear little virgins . . . I can't understand you, Peter – or Helen.

PETER. I know you can't, Joan.

JOAN. But how awful for you, you poor darlings! You must do something about it at once.

PETER. Well, I'm trying as hard as I can to get a job.

JOAN. What do people need to get married on nowadays?

PETER. Oh, I don't know. About £10 per week.

JOAN. (*With some difficulty.*) If it's simply a question of that, I know David would be awfully glad to make things all right.

PETER. Oh!

JOAN. (*Hastily.*) I mean he'd be awfully glad to raise your salary or whatever you call it to, say, ten pounds a week. You could still go on working here, you see, and it wouldn't really be like taking an allowance or anything –

PETER. (*Interrupting.*) Have you talked about this to David?

JOAN. Well, no, of course I haven't. But I know he'd be awfully glad –

PETER. It's terribly kind of you, Joan. Really, I'm most awfully grateful. But I'm afraid I couldn't possibly accept it.

JOAN. Think it over.

PETER. It's no good thinking it over. I could never accept it, really.

JOAN. Oh well, I knew you wouldn't.

PETER. You understand why, don't you?

JOAN. I couldn't understand less. But I still knew you wouldn't accept it.

PETER. I hope you don't think I'm an ungrateful swine.

JOAN. Don't be school-boyish, darling. You know, I don't think anything of the sort. I think you're a fool, that's all.

PETER. Yes, I suppose I am.

JOAN. Oh, well, don't let's say any more about it. (*She gets up and puts her glass down on the table.*) I wonder if I dare go in and see my glamorous husband. (*She looks towards the door.*) Is he conscious yet?

PETER. He's conscious all right.

JOAN. How's he feeling? Do you know?

PETER. I don't, I'm afraid. I haven't seen him yet.

JOAN. I've been a bit worried about him since he started that pain in his side a couple of days ago. I don't want him to go and die on me or anything.

PETER. He says it's only liver.

JOAN. I know, ducky, but that doesn't make it any better. Liver's the bogey of all of us.

PETER. He ought to go and see a doctor.

JOAN. Of course he ought, darling, but who the hell's going to get him to do it? He thinks all doctors are liars and thieves and bores. (*As an afterthought.*) So they are, of course.

PETER. Well, anyway, I don't think he can be feeling too bad this morning, because he's reading over that stuff we did last night.

JOAN. You know I don't think I shall ever forgive David for what he did last night. He woke me up at five to tell me all about his dreary book. He was awfully proud of himself for having worked a couple of hours on it, poor lamb. Tell me honestly, Peter, what do you think of it?

PETER. Of his book? (*Carefully.*) I think it's very good.

JOAN. I said honestly, darling.

PETER. Well, I think the subject's so uninteresting. I mean, who the hell wants to read a life of King Bomba of Naples? I mean, he's not an awfully important character, historically speaking, is he?

JOAN. Don't say that to David, or he'll kill you. As a matter of fact, I agree with you. I think King Bomba is torture.

PETER. But I'm not saying I don't think the book is good. I think it is. I think David's got a magnificent brain for history, if only he'd – (*He stops.*)

JOAN. If only he'd use it a bit more. Is that what you were going to say?

PETER. Yes, I was, as a matter of fact.

JOAN. You are a serious-minded little thing, aren't you?

PETER. (*Angrily.*) All right, I am. So what?

JOAN. So, nothing, darling. So nothing. Actually I think it's very good for David to have someone like you around. In fact, if you could get him to finish that book, I'd be eternally grateful.

PETER. (*Surprised.*) Really? Why?

JOAN. I don't know. I just think it would do David an awful lot of good to finish that book, dreary as it is.

PETER. (*After a slight pause.*) You surprise me sometimes, Joan.

JOAN. (*Vaguely.*) Do I, darling? I've no idea why.

A ring at the front door.

Oh, my God! People. I'm in no mood for people this morning. I think I'll go hide in David's room.

She moves towards DAVID*'s door and then, as if remembering something, darts towards the table and starts to pour herself out another drink.*

WILLIAMS *comes in.*

WILLIAMS. Mr and Miss Banner are here, madam.

JOAN. (*With a shriek.*) Mr Banner? Helen's got married, Peter. I told you she would.

PETER. It's her brother, I imagine. Still, I don't know what she thinks she's doing, bringing him round here.

JOAN. Nonsense, darling. Delighted to have him.

WILLIAMS. Shall I show them in here, madam?

JOAN. Yes, Williams.

    WILLIAMS *goes out.*

    You'll entertain them for me, won't you, Peter? (*At the door of* DAVID'*s room.*) I think you've got all you want there. (*She waves vaguely towards the drink table.*) If you want any more, just call Williams. (*She knocks on* DAVID'*s door and opens it.*) David, your loving wife seeks admittance.

DAVID. (*Off.*) Come in and shut the door. I don't like all that daylight.

JOAN. Why don't you pull up the blind?

    JOAN *goes in and shuts the door behind her, just as* WILLIAMS *enters, showing in* HELEN *and* GEORGE BANNER. HELEN *is about twenty,* GEORGE *about twenty-five.*

    WILLIAMS *goes out.*

HELEN. (*After a quick glance around the room.*) Hello, Peter!

    PETER *goes to her and kisses her.*

PETER. You're a little early, darling; that's lovely! Let's go and have lunch now.

HELEN. Don't let's go out just yet, Peter. I'll tell you why in a minute. You know my brother George, don't you?

GEORGE. Yes, we met once at Oxford. How are you?

PETER. Very well, thanks awfully.

    They shake hands.

    Are you still up?

HELEN. You're talking to Dr Banner, Peter.

PETER. Oh, really? Congratulations. So you got through all right.

GEORGE. By the skin of my teeth.

HELEN. (*Excitedly.*) Listen, Peter, is David up yet?

PETER. No, he's not. Why?

HELEN. I'll tell you. I want George to see him.

PETER. Oh! Well, I expect he'll be up quite soon –

HELEN. No, you don't understand. I want George to examine
him. You know – as a doctor.

PETER. You mean this is a sort of professional visit.

HELEN. No, no. He's doing it as a favour to me. You know
David's ill, Peter. He must be. He won't admit it, of course,
and he won't see a doctor, although I've – we've all begged
him to. So I thought I'd bring George along in the ordinary sort
of social way, and then he couldn't very well refuse to let
George have a look at him.

PETER. That's all you know of David. He'll be absolutely livid.

HELEN. Oh, no, he won't.

GEORGE *wanders over to the window and looks out.*

PETER. (*Bewildered.*) Helen, you must be mad to do this.

HELEN. Why?

PETER. If you knew David better, you'd realise he hates any sort
of interference; and, after all, what's it got to do with you?

HELEN. If anybody's as ill as David is, he ought to see a doctor.

PETER. He's not ill.

HELEN. Yes, he is. You've only got to take one look at him to
know there's something wrong with him.

PETER. You don't have to tell me what's wrong with him. I know:
Drink.

HELEN. Of course. That's why I want George to see him and tell
him just what it means for him to go on drinking as he is now.

PETER. I see. In other words, you've told your brother just what
he's to say to David.

HELEN. Yes, I have. If we can't stop him drinking any other way,
the only thing to do is to frighten him out of it.

PETER. You're taking rather a lot on yourself, aren't you?

HELEN. Don't be silly, Peter.

GEORGE *has been pretending not to hear the preceding
conversation. He now turns round from the window.*

GEORGE. I didn't know you could get a view like this in London.
It's more like New York.

PETER *and* HELEN *look round quickly and then back at each other.*

PETER. I'm sorry, Helen. It's only that you don't know David very well, and I'm afraid – (*He stops.*)

HELEN. Afraid of what, darling?

PETER. I'm afraid he'll be rude to you, or something, when he finds out about this.

HELEN. I'll take the risk, Peter.

GEORGE. What have I got myself into?

PETER. (*Unconvincingly.*) Oh, well, I expect it will be all right. Now I've been told to entertain you. (*To* GEORGE.) What'll you have to drink?

GEORGE. I don't drink, thanks.

PETER. What about you, Helen?

HELEN. Not in the daytime, darling.

PETER. Well, anyway, let's sit down. David may be hours yet.

They find chairs.

(*After a pause.*) What's the news, Helen?

HELEN. Nothing much. Oh, I went after that job yesterday.

PETER. (*Eagerly.*) Oh yes. Any luck?

HELEN. I shouldn't think so. There were about five hundred other girls there, and they all looked appallingly efficient. Hundred words a minute girls, most of them, I should say; so I must have looked pretty silly with my sixty. I wish to God they'd taught me to type at school, instead of how to write Greek verse.

GEORGE. Don't show off, Helen. You know you don't know a word of Greek.

HELEN. I did when I was at school.

A ring at the door.

Oh, Lord, are they expecting anyone this morning?

PETER. I've no idea. But, you know, people are always dropping in here.

HELEN. Yes, the most awful people, too.

WILLIAMS *comes in.*

WILLIAMS. Mrs Browne and Mr Carter.

WILLIAMS *goes out after showing in* JULIA *and* CYRIL. JULIA *is an untidily-dressed, rather insignificant-looking woman of about thirty-five, whose manner and behaviour entirely belie her appearance.* CYRIL *is a very good-looking, very well-dressed young man in the early twenties.*

JULIA. (*Advancing on* HELEN.) Helen, darling. Heaven to see you. (*She kisses her and advances on* PETER.) Peter, my angel, how are you? (*She holds out her arms, and* PETER *has, perforce, to kiss her.*) You look lovelier every day, how do you do it?

HELEN. I don't think you've met my brother George.

JULIA. Oh, how do you do? Why haven't I met you before?

GEORGE. I've no idea.

They shake hands. PETER *surreptitiously wipes his mouth.*

JULIA. We've just got back from Le Touquet, practically this minute. I'm stinking. (*She sinks into a chair.*) We took a bottle of brandy up in the aeroplane with us and, of course, we had to finish it before we got to Croydon because of the customs.

CYRIL *has been standing, awkwardly twitching his immaculate clothes. The others are eyeing him, embarrassed, waiting to be introduced.*

We had the most torturous weekend. I can't tell you how awful it was. I lost my drawers.

GEORGE. (*Feeling something is expected of him.*) Oh, dear.

JULIA. It was really torturous. I couldn't do a thing right. If I had eight the other man always had nine. I mean, it got to be a joke.

CYRIL *coughs suggestively, trying to imply his wish to he introduced.* JULIA *looks at him.*

Cyril played boule, and made a little money, didn't you, Cyril? I must tell you – I had an awful scene with a horrible little man who bancoed a bank of mine. You see, I made a perfectly natural mistake – I gave him three cards or something – you know the sort of thing that happens to you when you've had a couple of drinks – and he called me a drunken old bitch. In French, too, which made it worse. Of course, I couldn't stand that, so I –

CYRIL *coughs again, nodding his head towards the others.*

I hope you didn't catch cold in that aeroplane, Cyril.

CYRIL. (*In strong Cockney tones.*) I 'aven't been interdoosed yet.

JULIA. Oh, I'm so sorry. This is Mr – (*She hesitates.*) Hell, I always forget.

CYRIL. Carter.

JULIA. Mr Carter.

HELEN AND PETER. How do you do?

CYRIL. Quite well, thanks.

JULIA. (*To* PETER.) Ducky, what about a tingy-wingy little dinkey-boo?

PETER. I beg your pardon?

JULIA. A drink, for God's sake.

PETER. Oh, yes, I'm sorry. (*He goes to drink table.*) What would you like?

JULIA. Brandy I suppose. I started on it.

PETER. (*To* CYRIL) And you?

CYRIL. Same please.

JULIA. I suppose those monsters, Joan and David, aren't up yet?

PETER. Er, no. I don't think they are. (*He hands her a brandy and soda.*)

JULIA. Was there a party last night?

PETER. Not a party.

JULIA. Angel child! God, you are heaven to look at, Peter.

    PETER *turns his back abruptly.*

    I hope you realise how lucky you are, Helen.

HELEN. Yes, I suppose I am.

    PETER *gives* CYRIL *his drink.*

CYRIL. Thanks, I'm sure.

    JOAN *comes out of* DAVID's *room.*

JOAN. Julia, you old cow. How are you?

JULIA. Drunk as a fly, darling. How are you?

    JULIA *and* JOAN *embrace.*

    You've met Cyril, haven't you?

JOAN. Have I met you, Cyril?

CYRIL. Yus. We went out last Thursday.

JOAN. How are you? Julia, my pet. I'm sure you've got everything in the world to tell me. Come into my room and talk to me while I'm having my bath.

JULIA. (*Getting up.*) Darling, I've got the most heavenly bit of dirt to give you. You know Arthur Parke-Weston, don't you?

JOAN. The one who shot that girl and got off?

JULIA. Yes, that's the one. (*At the door of* JOAN's *room.*) Come on, Cyril. (*To* JOAN.) All right, Joan; he won't look. I'll put him in the corner with his face to the wall. Well, my dear, he was at Le Touquet with – Cyril!

They go into JOAN's *room.* CYRIL *follows gloomily to the door.*

CYRIL. (*At door, feelingly.*) Oh, Lord! (*He follows them in.*)

GEORGE. (*After a considerable pause.*) Well, well.

HELEN. (*Laughing.*) Poor George! Were you shocked?

GEORGE. No, of course I wasn't. As a matter of fact, it was rather exciting. It was the first time I'd ever met those sort of people. I'd only read about them before.

PETER. Yes, I know the feeling. Whenever I meet Julia Browne or any of the gang that come roaring into this flat, I always feel they don't really exist.

HELEN. They don't really.

GEORGE. What have I just seen, then? A couple of phantasmagoria?

HELEN. Oh, George, what a lovely word!

GEORGE. I'll never be able to say it again, don't worry.

PETER. Actually what Helen meant was that these people are all so busy putting on an act they haven't got time to be themselves.

GEORGE. Perhaps they haven't got any selves.

HELEN. Oh, yes, I think they have; quite nice ones, too, some of them. I wish I knew why they were always so ashamed of showing them.

PETER. They think it's boring to be one's self. That's their favourite word – boring. (*To* HELEN.) John said I was a bore this morning just because I was trying to get a decent job.

HELEN. You know what the trouble with these people is really, don't you? They've got too much money.

GEORGE. It's a trouble I wouldn't mind having myself, then.

HELEN. No, really I think it's rather pathetic. They might all have been quite different if they'd been given a proper chance. It must be awful having to grow up without having to work.

DAVID opens the door of his room. He is in flannels and tweed coat, which he is, at the moment, slipping on. He is thirty-eight. He has some typescript in his hand.

DAVID. (*As he opens the door.*) Peter, Leopold I wasn't King of Belgium, he was King of the Belgians. You ought to know that. (*He comes into the room.*) Hullo, Helen!

HELEN. Hello, David! This is my brother George.

DAVID. (*Shaking hands.*) How do you do? Haven't you got a drink?

GEORGE. I don't want one now, thanks awfully.

DAVID *goes to the drink table.*

DAVID. Nobody else?

PETER *and* HELEN *shake their heads.*

DAVID *pours himself out a whisky and soda.* HELEN *watches him anxiously.*

HELEN. How do you feel this morning, David?

DAVID. Just about as well as could be expected, I should say.

HELEN. You haven't got that pain again, have you?

DAVID. What pain?

HELEN. That pain you had yesterday in your side.

DAVID. Oh, that. That's only that old wound I got in the Crimea. I only feel it when it rains.

HELEN. (*Impatiently.*) David, please –

DAVID. Will you forgive me if I talk shop for a moment? (*He turns his back and goes over to* PETER.) Peter, one of us must have been very drunk last night.

PETER. (*A trifle sulkily.*) I wasn't.

DAVID. Then I was.

PETER. Why? Don't you like that stuff we did last night?

DAVID. As they say so expressively in America – it stinks.

He hands PETER *the typescript.*

PETER. (*Glancing through it.*) I thought it read rather well.

DAVID. That's just the trouble with it. It reads too well, like imitation Hector Bolitho.

PETER. Well, you're writing it to be read, aren't you?

DAVID. Not by the sort of people who read Hector Bolitho.

PETER. He's a good writer.

DAVID. I'm not saying he's not. But I'm afraid we'll have to work on that chapter again.

PETER. All right. This afternoon?

DAVID. No, not this afternoon. Some time. (*Turning round.*) Well, Helen, did you get that job you were after?

HELEN. No, I don't think so.

DAVID. Well, you'd probably have loathed it, anyway.

He sinks heavily into an armchair. HELEN *comes rather timidly up to him.*

HELEN. David, I've got something to ask you – a kind of favour.

DAVID. Anything, short of my honour.

HELEN. David, my brother George is a doctor – (*She stops.*)

DAVID. (*Politely.*) Oh, really? (*To* GEORGE.) What a delightful life that must be.

HELEN. (*Desperately.*) Don't you think, as he's here, it might be a good chance of getting him to have a look at you, just to see if there *is* anything the matter with you? I mean, there probably isn't, but it's a good thing to make sure, don't you think?

There is a pause. DAVID *gazes at her.*

DAVID. (*Mildly.*) You shouldn't do things like this, Helen.

HELEN. It wasn't a plot or anything. George happened to be here, and I suddenly thought –

DAVID. (*Smiling.*) Just a sudden inspiration. I see. What does Dr Banner think about the idea?

GEORGE. Oh, I'd be quite willing to take a look at you, if you're worried about yourself in any way.

DAVID. I'm not in the least worried about myself.

GEORGE. (*Acting his part rather badly.*) Still, from what Helen's told me about you, things aren't functioning quite as well as they should be, eh? Probably there's just a little something wrong with the old works which we can put right in a couple of seconds.

DAVID. (*Shaking his head sadly.*) The bedside manner so early in life.

GEORGE. Of course, if you don't want me to examine you –

DAVID. It's very kind of you to make the offer, but, quite frankly, I don't think it's worth your trouble.

GEORGE. Very well, then. (*He looks at his watch.*) I ought to be going. I've got a lunch date.

HELEN *stops him with a gesture.*

HELEN. David, please. As a favour to me.

Pause. DAVID *finishes his drink and puts it down.*

DAVID. As a favour to Helen, will you please examine me, Dr Banner?

GEORGE. (*After a glance a*t HELEN.) I've already said I would.

DAVID. We'd better go into my room.

GEORGE. Right.

DAVID. (*Holding open the door of his room,* GEORGE *going towards it.*) What Helen wants you to say, of course, is that I'm drinking myself to death, so I ought to tell you before we start that if you say that, I shan't believe it.

GEORGE. (*As he goes in.*) If I say it, it'll be true.

DAVID. I still won't believe it.

GEORGE *and* DAVID *go into* DAVID*'s room. There is a silence between* HELEN *and* PETER.

HELEN. You see, it wasn't so frightening, Peter, was it?

PETER. I'm amazed; honestly I am. I swear to you that if Joan or I had done what you've done we'd have had our heads bitten off.

HELEN. Oh, David isn't the ogre you think he is.

She looks at his door with a slight smile. PETER *finds this annoying.*

PETER. Anyway, it's not going to do any earthly good. If you think you're going to stop him drinking by frightening him you're on the wrong horse.

HELEN. (*Still with the self-satisfied smile.*) We'll see.

PETER. Darling, do stop trying to look like Florence Nightingale.

HELEN. I didn't know I was. I'm sorry.

She goes to a chair and sits.

PETER. I can't understand what all the fuss is about. Why pick on David? Why not try and stop Joan from drinking – or John, if it comes to that – or that Browne woman?

HELEN. Because David's worth more than all the rest of them put together.

PETER. Who says so?

HELEN. I say so. Why do you think he drinks, Peter?

PETER. How the hell should I know? Because he likes the taste of whisky, I suppose.

HELEN. You see, you've known David all your life, and you don't know him at all, really.

PETER. While you, with your fine womanly intuition, have only known him a month and can see right through him, I suppose?

HELEN. Peter, it seems silly to start a quarrel on a lovely day like this.

PETER. (*Sitting.*) It certainly seems silly to start a quarrel about David.

He says the name disparagingly. HELEN *is almost stung into saying something, but she checks herself. She comes over and sits on the arm of his chair.* PETER *takes her hand.*

HELEN. You haven't told me your news yet.

PETER. I haven't any.

HELEN. Something must have happened to you since Thursday.

PETER. Oh, wait a minute. (*He turns and looks up at her.*) Darling, we came very near to being married this morning.

HELEN. Did we?

PETER. I had a ten pound a week job offered me.

HELEN. What, in that bank?

PETER. No. If it had been in that bank I wouldn't have turned it down. No, it was here, I'm afraid.

HELEN. How do you mean, here?

PETER. An offer was made to me to go on working here at ten pounds a week – just so that I could marry you. (*He pats her hand.* HELEN *withdraws it suddenly.*)

HELEN. (*After a slight pause.*) You mean David offered you that? (PETER *feels her slight tenseness, and turns to look up at her.*)

PETER. (*Casually.*) Yes.

HELEN *gets up and wanders over to the window.*

Of course, I turned it down.

HELEN. (*Listlessly.*) Why did you do that?

PETER. You wouldn't like us to get married on charity from David, would you?

HELEN. No. No, I wouldn't.

PETER. (*Casually.*) Still, it was damned nice of him, wasn't it?

HELEN. (*Equally casually now.*) Yes it was.

.

JULIA, CYRIL *and* JOAN *come out of* JOAN's *room.* JOAN *is still in her dressing-gown.* JULIA *is speaking.*

JULIA. No, darling. I'm afraid I can't. I'd love to stay, but Cyril and I are having lunch with Moya Lexington.

JOAN. Oh, is she out of the home now? I didn't know.

JULIA. My dear, she's been out a month.

JOAN. How is she?

JULIA. Oh, she's quite all right again now.

JOAN. Isn't she – ? (*She makes a slight gesture, as of a hypodermic entering her arm.*)

JULIA. Of course she is, darling, but it's all under government supervision. They allow her as much every day as would ordinarily wipe out a whole army. It's supposed to be getting less and less, of course. In about 1980 she'll probably be down to the normal dose. Well, I must fly. I'm meeting her at the Fitzroy, and you know where that is – in the wilds of Bloomsbury.

JOAN. Don't be so rude about Bloomsbury. You were very glad to have a bed-sit there before you married that pulp merchant.

JULIA. (*Hating* JOAN.) Ah, but Bloomsbury was Bloomsbury then.

JOAN. What is is now? Chiswick?

JULIA. Do you remember that party I gave when everyone came dressed as the character in history they'd liked to have been?

JOAN. Yes, it was heaven.

JULIA. David came as the Prince Regent – and you – what were you?

JOAN. (*Embarrassed.*) I don't remember.

JULIA. I do. You came as Jane Austen. That was rather drab of you, dear. You should have thought of something better than that. God, it was a heavenly party. Martin Hedges fell downstairs and broke his leg. Do you remember?

JOAN. Oh, yes. He tried to kill himself, didn't he, or something. Or was he pushed? I can't remember.

JULIA. He was stinking, and fell, darling, that was all. Well, I must say goodbye. (*She embraces* JOAN.) Goodbye, Joan; heaven to see you again. I'm coming to that party of yours on the fifteenth. When's that, now? I mustn't forget. It's a week from today, isn't it?

JOAN. That's right. It isn't really a party. Just a few old friends.

JULIA. It'll be like old times, I'm sure. Cyril, remember a week from today – party here, ten o'clock.

CYRIL. O.K.

JULIA. (*Turning on* HELEN *and kissing her.*) Goodbye, Helen. Lovely seeing you.

HELEN. Goodbye, Julia.

JULIA. (*Turning on* PETER.) Goodbye, you Ganymede, you.

PETER. Oh, for God's sake –

JULIA. Cyril, run downstairs and get a taxi.

CYRIL. O.K. (*He turns at the door and bows, in stately fashion, from the waist.*) Goodbye all.

  CYRIL *goes out.*

JULIA. I shall be late for Moya. She'll be furious.

JOAN. Give her my love.

JULIA. I will, darling. By the way, have you heard the latest Moya story?

JOAN. No.

  PETER *exits.*

JULIA. It's perfectly true. I got it from Moya herself. Apparently, when she was in her heyday – you know, before she went into the home – she attended a civic luncheon given in her honour – famous airwoman upholding honour of Great Britain and all that – and she sat next to the Lord Mayor. Well, my dear, half way through the proceedings she felt she needed a shot, so she took out her hypodermic and stuck it into her leg. Only it wasn't her leg – it was the Lord Mayor's, and he screamed and passed out flat and had to be carried out. It's a heavenly story, don't you think? You must get her to tell you about it sometime.

JOAN. I certainly will. Goodbye, Julia.

JULIA. Goodbye, darling. Give my love to David.

  They go through door left and out into the hall, where they are still visible and audible.

By the way, what do you think of Cyril?

JOAN. I think he's torture.

JULIA. Yes, I suppose he is. Well, see you today week.

  JULIA *goes out.* JOAN *closes the front door after her, then comes back into the room and gets herself another drink.*

JOAN. Julia's pretty hard to take in the morning, don't you think?

HELEN. She's pretty hard to take any time, if you ask me.

JOAN. Helen. I have a nasty feeling I haven't said 'Good morning' to you yet.

HELEN. (*Smiling.*) You've cut me dead twice already today.

JOAN. Darling, I'm so sorry. Julia never gives one a moment for the social amenities. How are you? (*She kisses her.*) Oh, my God! I must have cut your brother too and he's gone.

HELEN. No, he hasn't gone.

JOAN. Oh, is he looking at the geography of the flat?

HELEN. No. He's in there with David. (*She points to* DAVID*'s door.*) He's a doctor, you know, and he's having a look at David to see if he can find out what that pain is. (*Slight pause.*) Don't you think it's a good idea?

JOAN. Whose idea was it? David's?

HELEN. What do *you* think?

JOAN. It was your idea, of course.

HELEN. After all, that pain must mean something.

JOAN. It's probably wind.

HELEN. Even so, I think one ought to find out for certain. And you know what David's like about doctors.

JOAN. Oddly enough, Helen, I do. I know quite a lot about David, though you mightn't think it. I've only been married to him for twelve years.

HELEN. I should have asked you about it before I did it. I'm sorry.

JOAN. (*Mildly.*) Oh, no. Why should you?

HELEN. If I'd known you'd mind I wouldn't have done it.

JOAN. Oh yes, you would.

HELEN. All right then, I would. I think someone ought to try and stop David from drinking himself to death – even if his own wife does stand by and do nothing.

HELEN *is immediately frightened of what she has said.* JOAN *however, seems far from upset.*

JOAN. You might have gone further than that, and said she even encourages him. (*She takes a gulp of her drink just to show what she means.*) Don't let's be bores, Helen darling, I'm not taking any attitude about this. I think it's very sweet of you to take all this trouble – especially about someone you hardly know.

HELEN *is silent.* JOAN *puts her glass down on the table and stretches herself.*

(*Looking at the clock.*) God, it's late. We'll be eating in about ten minutes. I'd better go and put some clothes on. (*She wanders over to the radio-gramophone in the corner.*) I wonder if there's any gay music on the air. (*She twiddles knobs and gets a dance band playing some modern swing numbers. She listens to it for a few seconds and then switches it off.*)

I think these modern tunes are torture. Let's have the gramophone. (*She puts on an old and rather scratchy record of 'Avalon'.*) God, what this tune means to me! I suppose you weren't born when they were playing it?

HELEN. Oh, yes. I remember it quite well. My nurse used to sing it.

JOAN. She had good taste. Are you a war-baby?

HELEN. No, a peace-treaty baby. I was born in December 1918.

JOAN. Still that counts as a war-baby – I mean if you work it out backwards. God, this tune! It tears me to shreds.

JOAN *goes into her room humming it.* HELEN, *left alone, lights a cigarette. The record comes to an extra scratchy bit and repeats itself indefinitely.*

HELEN *impatiently puts out her cigarette, goes over to the gramophone and switches it off.* GEORGE *comes out of* DAVID*'s room and closes the door behind him.*

HELEN. (*Eagerly.*) Well?

GEORGE. Well I've told him that if he doesn't give up drinking altogether he'll be dead pretty soon.

HELEN. (*Conspiratorially.*) Good. Well done, George. Did he take any notice of what you said?

GEORGE. I don't know. He showed a certain polite interest – that was about all.

HELEN. He didn't suspect anything, did he?

GEORGE. How do you mean?

HELEN. Did you sound convincing? I mean, did you make him believe that what you said was the truth?

GEORGE. You don't seem to understand, Helen. What I told him was the truth.

Pause. HELEN *puts her hand up to her mouth with an involuntary gesture.*

HELEN. What?

GEORGE. He's got very obvious symptoms of the beginnings of acute cirrhosis of the liver.

HELEN. But, George, are you sure you're right?

GEORGE. I know I'm right. That's to say unless everything I've learned up to now has been crazy. Obviously, he ought to be looked at by someone with more experience. But equally obviously, he won't do it, so you'll just have to believe me.

HELEN. If he gave up drink – entirely – would he be all right?

GEORGE. And if he sticks to the diet I gave him – I think he would, yes.

They go through the door left, and out into the hall, where they are visible.

Well, I've really got to go now. I want you to know I wouldn't go through what I've been through this morning for anyone else in the world.

DAVID comes out of his room. He is in the same clothes as before, and smoking a cigarette. He stretches himself idly and goes to the drink table.

HELEN. (*Outside in the hall.*) I'm terribly grateful to you. Really I am.

GEORGE. That's all right. It might lead to some good rich patients. Goodbye, Helen. Behave yourself.

HELEN. Goodbye, George.

She closes the front door after him. DAVID has, meanwhile, poured himself out a whisky and soda. HELEN comes back into the room and sees him. She crosses the room quickly and knocks the glass out of his hand as he is raising it to drink.

Stop that, you damned fool!

DAVID's first emotion is obviously violent anger. He controls himself quickly.

DAVID. Really, Helen, I wish you wouldn't play tennis with my best glasses. Besides, you've made a nasty mess on a very nice carpet. Ring the bell, will you?

HELEN crosses and rings the bell. DAVID picks up the glass and then goes to the table, takes another glass and pours himself out another drink.

HELEN. (*Helplessly.*) David, for God's sake . . .

HELEN makes a motion towards him. He turns to face her with a glass in his hand.

DAVID. Now, you're not going to repeat that little gesture. It was effective the first time, but it might lose its point if you do it again.

HELEN. Put that drink down, you fool.

DAVID. I intend to.

HELEN *is going towards him as* WILLIAMS *comes in. She stops.*

HELEN. You're mad.

DAVID. Listen, Helen. I believe your story. I believe your brother really thinks I've got cirrhosis of the liver and that I'll be dead pretty soon.

HELEN. You think he's wrong, then?

DAVID. He may easily be right, but then I've been told so often by doctors that I'm killing myself by drinking that what your brother told me this morning only brought it a little nearer.

HELEN. (*Desperately.*) Don't you want to go on living?

DAVID. I must have notice of that question. It's a little difficult to answer offhand.

HELEN. (*Changing her tactics.*) Oh, David, I understand you so much better than you think. I know why you drink and believe me, I sympathise. But that's all the more reason why –

DAVID. (*Impatiently.*) You're an incurably romantic little girl. I drink because I like it and because I always have. Those are the only two reasons I know and they're good enough for me to go on drinking, in spite of the horrid warning of your doctor brother.

HELEN *shakes her head.* DAVID *rises impatiently and walks over to her.*

Now, will you kindly get this into your head. I am not a pathological case. I have no neuroses or repressions or fixations rattling about inside me. Nor did my mother drop me on my head when I was a baby. I am a perfectly normal human being, and I like drinking. Is that enough?

HELEN. No, it isn't.

DAVID. All right, what else?

HELEN. The war . . .

DAVID. (*Clutching his head.*) Oh, Lord, the war! The horrors of the trenches – the blood, the mud – my best friend killed in my arms – the memory of it haunting me still. Helen, will you try to get this into your novelettish little mind. I wasn't even in the war. I missed it by a whole bloody month.

HELEN. I don't care. I still say it's the war that makes you lead such a fantastic life.

DAVID. I don't admit it is fantastic. Anyway, what's the war got to do with it?

HELEN. You see, when you were eighteen you didn't have anybody of twenty-two or twenty-five or thirty or thirty-five to help you, because they'd been wiped out. And anyone over forty you wouldn't listen to, anyway. The spotlight was on you and you alone, and you weren't even young men; you were children.

DAVID. I like your disdain of eighteen from the Olympian heights of twenty. It's very pleasing.

HELEN. Oh, I'm a child, too. I admit it.

DAVID. All right, then. Go on. What did we do with this spotlight?

HELEN. You did what any child would do. You danced in it.

DAVID. Now you're going whimsical. You mustn't do that. How do you mean, we danced in it?

HELEN. You know perfectly well what I mean. You had a hell of a good time – with all the money in the world and everyone beaming on you and applauding your antics.

DAVID. (*Thoughtfully.*) It was a little more than that. You're putting it at its lowest terms. At its highest it had the value of a gesture.

HELEN. (*Excitedly.*) I know. But a gesture that hasn't any meaning now – so you should stop making it.

DAVID. (*Recalled to himself.*) That's very perspicacious of you; very undergraduette.

HELEN. Oh, David, you do see what I've been trying to tell you, don't you?

DAVID. Yes, that I'm a drunken waster.

HELEN. Oh, David, that's not what I mean. Drinking is your escape from your life. You hate your life – so you drink.

Pause. DAVID *turns suddenly away from her and sits down.*

DAVID. My dear Helen, I'm very satisfied with my life.

He does not look at her as he says this. HELEN *comes behind his chair and looks down at him.*

HELEN. Why are all of you always trying to go back? Why does Joan play fifteen-year-old records on the gramophone? Why do you all talk of nothing but the old days and the old parties and the things you all used to do and say? Why?

DAVID. (*Sulkily.*) You tell me. You're bound to know the answer.

He still refuses to look at her.

HELEN. (*After a pause.*) What would you most have liked to have been in life, David?

DAVID. What I am now.

HELEN. Supposing that were impossible . . .

DAVID. (*After a pause, in a low voice.*) I don't know. I've no idea.

HELEN. I think you'd have liked to have been a historian, a great biographer. (*Pause.*) Wouldn't you?

DAVID. (*Murmuring.*) I suppose it's possible.

Pause.

HELEN. I think you'd like to be able to look forward, instead of always looking back.

DAVID *does not answer her.* HELEN *puts her hand out and gently touches his arm.*

(*Quietly*). You can start again, you know.

DAVID. (*In the same tone.*) No, I can't.

HELEN. With someone helping you, I think you can.

DAVID *says nothing. He stares in front of him.* HELEN *gently takes the glass of whisky from him.* DAVID *makes no effort to stop her. She takes it over to the window and throws it out.*

DAVID. (*Gently.*) My hat! You've got a nerve. You've probably given someone down there a shower of whisky.

HELEN. (*Smiling.*) There's never anybody down there in that courtyard.

DAVID. Why didn't you pour it in the flower-pot?

HELEN. It might have killed the flowers.

JOAN *comes out of her room, dressed. She looks from* DAVID *to* HELEN. *Then she picks up the cloth from the table where* HELEN *has dropped it.*

JOAN. What's this doing here, for God's sake?

HELEN. (*Gaily.*) All right, I'll take it and give it to Williams. We had a bit of an accident with a glass of whisky.

JOAN. Where's Peter? Has he deserted you?

HELEN. No, he's in his room. I'll go and pull him out. I'm hungry.

HELEN *goes out.*

JOAN *looks after* HELEN *thoughtfully, and then back at* DAVID, *who has not changed his position.*

JOAN. What did that brother of hers say about you?

DAVID. (*Not having listened.*) What?

JOAN. You know, that doctor man. What did he say about you?

DAVID. Oh, nothing. He said it was wind. (*He gets up and goes to the window.*)

JOAN. (*Showing relief, but not in her voice.*) That's what I thought it was.

DAVID. I knew it was.

JOAN. He's very young. Does he know enough to be sure?

DAVID. Oh, I expect so. Anyway, there's nothing the matter with me. Don't fuss.

JOAN. It was pretty good nerve of Helen's, asking him round here.

DAVID. Yes, it was, wasn't it?

JOAN. You know, that girl's so crazily in love with you it isn't funny – or hadn't you noticed?

DAVID. Yes, I had noticed. (*He wanders over to the piano.*)

JOAN. Do you think Peter has?

DAVID. I don't know. I don't think it matters much, do you? (*He starts to strum a few bars of 'Dinah'.*)

JOAN. No, I suppose not. She's only got a sort of romantic school-girlish thing about you. She'll get over it very easily.

DAVID *goes on playing.* WILLIAMS *comes in.*

WILLIAMS. Luncheon is served, madam.

JOAN. Thank you, Williams.

WILLIAMS *goes out.*

I'd better go and pull that hangover hog out of his bed.

JOAN *goes out.* DAVID *changes 'Dinah' to Chopin. After a few seconds* HELEN *comes in.* DAVID *does not hear her. She stands behind him.* PETER *follows her in.*

PETER. David, if you don't want me this afternoon for anything, I'd like to take Helen to a cinema.

DAVID, *after a quick look round, has changed Chopin back to 'Dinah'.*

DAVID. What are you going to see?

PETER. 'The Life of Victor Hugo', with Paul Muni.

DAVID. What a hellish way of spending an afternoon.

HELEN. How are you going to spend it?

DAVID. Asleep, I hope.

PETER. Do you mind, David?

    DAVID *gets up from the piano.*

DAVID. No, of course not.

    JOHN *and* JOAN *come in.*

JOHN. It's an indignity being woken up for stew.

JOAN. You take what's given you and like it.

DAVID. Good morning, John.

JOHN. I thought I'd seen you before today.

DAVID. Only in your dreams.

PETER. Helen, we'd better be going.

JOHN. Are you two going out to lunch?

HELEN. Yes, we are.

JOHN. You know what's good for you.

JOAN. Why don't you go with them?

JOHN. I might, if they'd pay for me. Where are you going?

HELEN. Lyons' Corner House.

JOHN. That quaint little restaurant in Coventry Street? I've heard of it. The food's so good and the manager's so attentive.

PETER. I gather you're not coming with us?

JOHN. You gather right, my child.

PETER. Come on, Helen. Goodbye, everyone.

    PETER *goes out.*

HELEN. (*At door.*) Goodbye, David.

DAVID. Goodbye, Helen.

    HELEN *follows* PETER *out.*

JOHN. (*To* DAVID.) Why do you rate a special goodbye?

DAVID. I've no idea.

JOAN. (*At drink table.*) Get yourselves drinks, everyone, and bring them in to lunch with you.

JOHN. Hell, that means there's no wine for lunch.

JOAN. We can open a bottle for you, if you like.

JOHN. (*Politely.*) Oh, no, that's quite all right. I *prefer* gin.

JOAN and JOHN are pouring themselves out drinks.

Aren't these young people bores? Lyons' Corner House! I ask you.

JOAN. Why do you keep on talking about young people, blast you? We're all young, aren't we, David? Here. (*She hands him a whisky and soda. He takes it and puts it down on the table. JOAN goes to gramophone.*) Let's have some music during lunch, shall we?

JOHN. No.

JOAN. Don't be a bore. You know I like it. (*She puts on the same record as before.*)

JOHN. Oh, this tune I like. It has poignant memories for me.

JOAN. It has for me, too.

JOHN. Do you remember when this tune first came out, and they played it at that party of Arthur Power's without stopping for a whole evening?

JOAN. (*Going towards the door.*) That was a good party. Will you ever forget Johnnie Benson, dressed in literally nothing, swinging on that chandelier, and all the old dowagers looking up at him through their lorgnettes.

JOHN. Poor Johnnie.

JOAN. Yes, poor Johnnie. Hell, it was an accident, that thing. The balustrade gave way. Come on. Lunch.

JOAN goes out. DAVID, who has been watching JOHN and JOAN thoughtfully, follows her out. JOHN goes to the gramophone.

JOHN. If we're going to hear this thing at all we'd better have it full strength.

He switches it on full, and then sees DAVID's drink untouched on the table. He picks it up.

(*Shouting.*) Hey, David, you've forgotten your drink.

He follows them out. The record plays for a few seconds and then reaches the spot where it begins to repeat itself.

Curtain.

Act Two, Scene One

Scene. The same. A week later. About four o'clock in the afternoon.
JOHN *is lying on the sofa, reading a book which, from the vivid
picture on the cover, is evidently a thriller.* PETER *is at his typewriter in the corner.* DAVID *is pacing up and down with a large
notebook open in his hand.*

DAVID. (*Dictating hesitantly.*) It was a time when Europe still lay
under the dark shadow cast by the giant figure of Prince
Metternich; when the twin forces of nationalism and liberalism
had not yet dared to show their heads . . .

PETER *types this out carefully, then turns round.*

PETER. Is that right?

DAVID. Is what right?

PETER. Twin forces showing their heads. And then 'dark shadow'
isn't very good is it?

DAVID (*Bad-tempered.*) Peter, I'd be awfully grateful if you'd
remember that your job is to take down what I dictate. When I
need a collaborator I'll tell you.

PETER. I'm sorry.

He turns back to his typewriter.

Pause. DAVID *rubs his forehead.*

DAVID. All right. Say, 'The twin forces of liberalism and
nationalism had not yet begun to make themselves felt.' And
cross out 'dark'. Just say 'shadow'.

PETER *makes the necessary correction.* DAVID *continues to
pace up and down.*

PETER. (*As he finishes.*) Right.

DAVID. The King of Naples sat securely on his throne, as yet
unsuspecting of the tremendous stirrings that were later –

JOHN. (*Suddenly.*) My God, it was the Home Secretary, after all.

DAVID. (*Startled.*) What?

JOHN. Do you remember, I said I thought it was the Home
Secretary who did it, and then I thought it was too obvious, so

it must be his mother. But now it turns out to be the Home Secretary after all. Carstairs had been blackmailing him because, before he was Home Secretary, he had stolen an Etruscan vase –

DAVID. (*Furious.*) Damn you, John. How the hell do you expect me to do any work with you interrupting me every second?

JOHN. I haven't interrupted you every second. I've hardly interrupted you at all.

DAVID. Well, shut up, for God's sake.

JOHN. (*Hurt.*) I thought you'd like to hear who did it. I think it's funny it being the Home Secretary after all.

DAVID. (*Shouting.*) It isn't in the least funny. Shut up.

> JOHN *shrugs his shoulders and throws away his book. He yawns and stretches himself and settles himself down comfortably in the cushions.*

Where had I got to, Peter?

PETER. (*Reading.*) ' . . . as yet unsuspecting of the tremendous stirrings that were later . . . '

DAVID. That were later to make themselves felt.

PETER. You can't say that. The twin forces made themselves felt in the last sentence.

DAVID. (*Viciously.*) God damn you!

PETER. Sorry. My mistake.

> *He turns back to his typewriter.* DAVID *closes his notebook with a slam and sits down.*

DAVID. We'd better stop. It's no good my trying to go on like this.

PETER. I'm sorry.

DAVID. That's all right. It's not your fault.

JOHN. (*Rising with dignity.*) If it's my presence that's disturbing you, I can easily go somewhere else.

PETER. You can't go in the dining-room, because they're getting it ready for the party. And your bedroom's being made into a place for hats and coats.

JOHN. (*With quiet martyrdom.*) I presume there's a vacant closet somewhere.

> *He makes as if to go.*

DAVID. Don't be an idiot, John. Sit down. It's my fault. I don't seem to be able to think straight this afternoon. My brain's gone ossified.

JOHN. Of course.

DAVID. Why 'of course'?

JOHN. It's all this going on the wagon that's done it. It's terrible what that does to the brain.

DAVID. How would *you* know about that?

JOHN. I knew someone else once who went on the wagon. Which reminds me . . . (*At the drink table.*) May I?

DAVID. Of course. I've never known you ask before.

JOHN. Your abstinence has made me self-conscious. (*He pours himself out a drink.*) He went mad.

DAVID. Who did?

JOHN. That other man I knew who went on the wagon.

PETER *has been packing up his typewriter. He now turns round.*

PETER. I'll go and type this stuff out in my room.

DAVID. You needn't bother to do it now, Peter.

PETER. It'd be a good thing to get it done before the party, don't you think? Then we'll be all set to start off again tomorrow.

DAVID. All right. It might be a good idea.

PETER *goes to the door.*

Oh, Peter, is Helen coming in this afternoon?

PETER. She didn't say anything to me about it. Why?

DAVID. I thought you were having dinner with her.

PETER. Yes, I am, but I'm meeting her at the Brasserie.

JOHN. At the what?

PETER. At the Brasserie Universelle.

JOHN. Dear God.

PETER. (*To* DAVID.) I'll shoot the stuff in to you before I go out. So long.

PETER *goes out.*

JOHN. (*Returning with his drink to the sofa.*) I'll bet you any money you like our little Peter has put his foot down and forbidden Helen to come round here any more.

DAVID. Why should he do that?

JOHN. He's not over-bright, but even he must have noticed the thing she's got about you.

DAVID *is silent.* JOHN *lies back in his favourite position.*

'No, Helen,' he's said to her: 'No, Helen, you mustn't go round there any more. He's a naughty, wicked man, and he'll take advantage of your purity and innocence to do naughty and wicked things to you.'

He looks up to see how DAVID *is taking this.*

Have you, by the way?

DAVID. Have I what?

JOHN. Done naughty wicked things to her?

DAVID. Sometimes I wonder why I don't kick you out of this flat right on your ear.

JOHN. Now, what am I to take that answer to mean? That you have, I suppose.

DAVID. No, damn you, I haven't.

JOHN. Isn't that extraordinary?

DAVID. Do you think so?

JOHN. I thought she was your type. Fair-haired, snub-nosed, ingénue. She's my type, anyway.

DAVID. I'm sure she'd be glad to know that.

JOHN. Come, come. You ought to be able to think of a better comeback than that. This giving up drinking hasn't done you any good.

DAVID. It's made me realise what bores some people are, anyway.

JOHN. Everybody's a bore unless you drink.

DAVID. No. Not everybody.

JOHN. Everybody. Now, what was I saying? Oh, yes, I was talking about Helen, wasn't I?

DAVID. You were, but if I were you I shouldn't go on talking about her.

JOHN. (*With wide eyes.*) Why on earth not?

DAVID *drops his slightly menacing attitude, finding it ridiculous.* JOHN *continues, enjoying himself.*

Now Helen's quite a nice little girl. Apart from the fact that she's what Huxley so daintily calls pneumatic, she's got some semblance of a mind – and that's a rare combination. Of course, she applies her mind wrong, like all her dreary generation. After two weeks of her alone one would probably go quite mad and kill her. Still, the fact remains, she's too good for Peter. In fact, I can't think of a better compliment to pay her, or you, if it comes to that, than to say that she deserves to be your girl friend.

DAVID. Listen, John. I'm serious. You're boring me to such an extent that I'm liable to do something very stupid if you don't stop.

JOHN. (*Innocently.*) Why, what have I said?

DAVID *angrily turns his back and picks up his notebook.* JOHN *watches him and chuckles.*

It doesn't seem possible, but it's evidently true, all the same.

DAVID. (*Turning angrily.*) What the hell do you mean by that?

JOAN *comes in from her room. She has a hat and coat on.*

JOAN. Are you two having what are popularly known as words?

JOHN. No, no. Just chatting amiably on this and that.

JOAN. I don't believe you. You've been annoying my glamorous husband. I can see it in his face.

JOHN. It's his conscience that's brought that blush to his cheeks – not I.

JOAN. You be careful, John. I'm not going to have you annoying my little David. He means a lot to me.

JOHN. About five thousand a year.

JOAN. Seven, when the dividends are good.

JOHN. I hope you're putting a lot by. You're not quite as young as you were, darling, and you never know when some gay, fresh-faced interloper mightn't oust you.

JOAN. Helen, for instance?

JOHN. Helen, for instance.

JOAN. Oh, I don't worry about that. Any hanky-panky, and I fly to my lawyers.

JOHN. You'd do pretty nicely on alimony.

JOAN. Not only alimony, darling – enticement. I should lead a lovely life in the south of France as a rich and glamorous divorcée.

JOHN. That'd be heaven. Then I could spend six months with you and six months with David.

DAVID. Don't worry. I wouldn't contest the custody of you. Joan could have you twelve months in the year.

JOHN. I should cry in court and you'd have to have me.

A ring at the front door.

JOAN. If that's Julia or anybody, you'll have to cope. I've got to go out.

DAVID. Oh, no. I can't cope with Julia, sober.

JOAN. Darling, I've got to go out. I'll be back in a second, though. I've only got to go across the street to Woolworth's to buy some glasses for the party.

DAVID. (*Gloomily.*) God, I wish we could put it off. If you knew how I hated the thought of it.

JOAN. I know exactly how you feel. It's hell having to go through a party without drinking. Why don't you go off the wagon, just for tonight?

DAVID. No, I won't do that. I'll just have to face it, that's all.

WILLIAMS *comes in.*

WILLIAMS. Miss Banner is here, madam.

There is a slight pause. JOHN *sits up.* DAVID *looks from* JOAN *to* JOHN.

DAVID. All right, Williams. Show her in here.

WILLIAMS *goes out.*

Peter said she wasn't coming round today.

JOHN. Peter apparently doesn't know everything.

WILLIAMS *re-enters, showing in* HELEN.

WILLIAMS. Miss Banner.

He goes out. HELEN *comes in. She is carrying a typescript folder under her arm.*

JOAN. Hello, Helen. Lovely to see you.

HELEN. I'm afraid this is an awful time to drop in. You're probably all upside down arranging for the party tonight.

JOAN. That's quite all right, darling. Only I've simply got to get to Woolworth's before closing time. Will you forgive me if I dash off? I'll be back in a second.

HELEN. Yes, of course. I'm terribly sorry –

JOAN. I don't know if Peter's in or not.

DAVID. He's working in his room.

JOAN. I'll get Williams to call him.

HELEN. No, don't do that. You see, it's David I really want to see.

JOAN. Oh! (*Fatuously.*) Well, he's here all right, aren't you,
David.

HELEN. I've got something to talk over with him. (*She taps the
typescript.*) Business, you might call it.

JOAN. It's just as well I'm going out, then. So long, Helen; see
you later.

HELEN. So long, Joan.

JOAN. If you want to talk business with David you can get rid of
that fat lump on the sofa by sending him into the dining-room
to do some work.

She goes out.

JOHN. She must have meant me.

HELEN. Oh, no John. How could she have meant you?

JOHN. Sarcasm in the young is most displeasing.

He goes towards the door of DAVID's *room.*

HELEN. The dining-room's that way.

She points in the other direction.

JOHN. You don't say.

He goes into DAVID's *room.*

DAVID. Hey, what are you going to do in my room?

JOHN. (*Sticking his head out.*) If you remember, my own room is
being transformed into a convenience, so I'm going to use
yours.

DAVID. Don't steal anything.

JOHN. (*With dignity.*) All I'm going to do is to lie on your bed
and read such letters as you've left lying about. Steal anything!
Really. Oh, well, I suppose it's my lot to be insulted.

He goes into DAVID's *room and shuts the door.* DAVID
laughs.

HELEN. Poor John. It must be an awful strain for him to keep
finding things to say that are going to make you laugh.

DAVID. (*Startled.*) Don't be so depressing, Helen.

HELEN. Sorry, David.

*She picks up the typescript, which she has laid down on the
table. Pause.*

DAVID. (*Eagerly.*) Well?

HELEN. Well, I've read it.

DAVID. You've been very quick.

HELEN. I stayed up practically all last night reading it.

Pause. DAVID *waits for her to go on, but she shows no disposition to do so.*

DAVID. I gather from your silence you don't like it.

HELEN. David, you did ask me to be absolutely honest, didn't you?

DAVID. Certainly.

HELEN. Then I'm afraid I've got to tell you that I think it's very bad.

DAVID. Oh.

HELEN. It's terribly hard for me, David. I'd love to say I thought it was good.

DAVID. What do you think is wrong with it?

HELEN. Everything.

DAVID. That's not exactly encouraging, is it?

HELEN. I don't mean it to be.

DAVID. You'd like me to scrap it?

HELEN. Yes. Scrap it altogether.

DAVID. (*Abruptly.*) That's impossible. I've put five years' work into it.

HELEN. Oh, no, you haven't. You've put a few weeks' work into it and spread it over five years. The trouble is in yourself, not in the book. Every fault in the book comes from your own laziness.

DAVID. Would you mind being a little more explicit?

HELEN. You haven't taken the trouble to read the documents and things you ought to, so all you've written is a lazy under-graduate's essay; rushing over the bits you haven't read up and stressing things that aren't important, just because you do happen to know about them.

DAVID. I didn't realise you knew so much about King Ferdinand of Naples.

HELEN. I don't know a damn thing about him – and I don't want to. He's a boring character, anyway.

DAVID. Then you are hardly competent to judge, are you?

HELEN. I can tell bad work when I see it.

DAVID. You're very clever.

HELEN. Just clear-sighted, that's all.

DAVID. (*Bitterly.*) Well, thank you very much for taking all this trouble. You've been very helpful.

HELEN. Is that my cue to go?

DAVID. I've got some things to do. I hope you don't mind.

He turns his back. HELEN *shrugs her shoulders, tosses the book on the sofa, and goes to the door.*

DAVID. I suppose you think I'm being childishly peevish with you, just because you don't happen to like my book.

HELEN. David, you did ask me to be honest –

DAVID. I didn't ask you to smash something altogether that does happen to mean quite a lot to me.

HELEN. Then I think it's wrong that the book should mean anything to you at all. Believe me, David, it's not worth a moment's thought. It's plain downright bad.

DAVID. (*Turning round, violently.*) Of course it's bad. Don't think you're telling me anything I don't know.

HELEN. Why did you give it to me to read, then? I don't understand.

DAVID. No, you don't. That's where I was so idiotically wrong. I thought you, of all people, would understand.

HELEN. (*Bewildered.*) I'm sorry, David. What have I done?

DAVID. All right, I'll tell you. You've talked a lot of bunk to me about the worthless life I'm leading and how I ought to change it into something better, haven't you?

HELEN. Everything I've ever said to you I've meant, David.

DAVID. Then why the hell do you have to go and cut the only link I've got between what I am now and what I'd like to be?

HELEN. (*Thoughtfully.*) I see. Oh, I see. I was a fool. You didn't want me to be honest about the book.

DAVID. I wanted you to lie as you've never lied before. I wanted you to tell me it was good – and I wanted to believe you. You were the only person in the world I wanted to hear that from.

HELEN. I didn't realise that book was only a symbol. I thought it was something more.

DAVID. How could it be anything more, when it's as bad as it is?

HELEN. It could be something more if you started it again.

DAVID. Don't make stupid jokes. They bore me.

HELEN. I think you're the most spineless, gutless creature in the world –

DAVID. I'm glad you've found me out.

HELEN. But I think I'm happier at this moment than I've ever been in my life.

DAVID. Why?

HELEN. Because now I know you need me.

DAVID stares at her and then turns back.

DAVID. You're wrong. I don't need you.

HELEN. I know you do now.

DAVID. (*His back to her.*) Why don't you go back to Peter and stop chasing me, for a second?

HELEN, smiling, goes up to him and puts her hand on his shoulder. He shakes himself free and turns to face her.

God, I wish I could hate you.

HELEN. Don't try, David; please don't try. I think I should die if you ever stopped being in love with me.

DAVID grips her shoulders and shakes her.

DAVID. Listen! Have I ever told you I was in love with you?

HELEN. You've never needed to. I've always known.

DAVID stares at her for a moment, then pulls her towards him and kisses her roughly.

HELEN. (*With complete calm.*) Why we haven't done that before, I don't know. Let's sit down.

She sits on the sofa and pulls him down beside her.

DAVID. (*Bewildered.*) Are you a human being, or are you a fish, by any chance?

She takes his hand and puts it over her heart.

HELEN. Does that feel like a human being?

DAVID. You'll die if it goes on like that.

HELEN. What about yours? (*She puts her hand over his heart.*) It's much slower than mine.

DAVID. It's more constant. Far more constant.

He makes an attempt to kiss her, but she pushes him away.

HELEN. David, please don't say things like that. It frightens me.

DAVID. Why?

HELEN. Because we happen to be in love with each other, and I don't like you to talk to me as if I were just another of those girls you sleep with one night and forget about the next. (*She pushes him to the far corner of the sofa.*) Come on, let's be sensible.

DAVID. (*Groaning.*) Oh, why did I have to fall in love with you? Why don't you leave me alone?

HELEN. I'm never going to leave you alone for the rest of your life.

DAVID. That's the most alarming thing I've ever heard.

HELEN. You bet it's alarming. It's bound to be alarming to be whisked back fifteen years and made to start one's life all over again.

DAVID. Is that what's going to happen to me?

HELEN. It is.

DAVID. With someone to help me, I could start again. You said that to me once, do you remember?

HELEN. And you said it wasn't possible. (*She takes his hand.*) But it is, David. I know it is.

DAVID (*Slowly.*) I hope it is. (*He bends down and kisses her hand.*) Oh, God, I hope it is.

HELEN. How is Joan going to take this?

DAVID *raises his head slowly and gazes at her.*

DAVID. Is that – necessary?

HELEN. Yes, David.

DAVID. It's a pretty horrible business to have to go through.

HELEN. I know it is, but it's got to be done. How do you think Joan will take it, David?

DAVID. (*Sitting up.*) She'll take it very well. (*He runs his hand through his hair.*) Oh God, I suppose I'll have to tell her.

HELEN. I'll tell her.

DAVID. I ought to.

HELEN. I'll tell her, David.

DAVID. You take a pretty gloomy view of my character, don't you?

HELEN. It's easier for me. (*After pause.*) David, she's not in love with you, is she?

DAVID. Good Lord, no.

HELEN. Has she ever been?

DAVID. I don't suppose so.

HELEN. Why did you get married, then?

DAVID. I've no idea. It was just one of those things that happened: we'd been having an affair. And then one day we were a bit drunk and we thought it might be fun to get married.

HELEN. You don't think she'll mind much, then, about us?

DAVID. She won't show any emotion at all. She'll probably be rude to you, in a vague sort of way.

HELEN. That's all right. I can cope with that. I like Joan. David, you are fond of her, aren't you?

DAVID. Of course, It's worked very well being married to her. We've got on marvellously, considering everything, for twelve years. What about Peter?

HELEN. He'll be terribly hurt. Poor Peter!

DAVID. I'd better tell him.

HELEN. (*Smiling.*) Darling! I love you when you're noble and self-sacrificing. It's so unlike you.

DAVID. Thank you so much.

HELEN. I'll tell Peter. I'm having dinner with him. I'll tell him tonight. (*Pause.* DAVID *gets up.*) What's the matter, David?

DAVID. Promise you won't leave me and go back to Peter.

HELEN. No, I won't. I only thought I was in love with Peter. I liked him. I still like him enormously. If I hadn't met you, I'd have married him.

DAVID. He's your age. You've got everything in common.

HELEN. (*Getting up.*) But having met you, I've no intention of marrying Peter. I've every intention of marrying you. So, David, will you please marry me? (*She holds out her hand to him.*)

DAVID. (*With a sigh.*) Yes, Helen. I'm afraid I will. (*He takes her hand and pulls her to him.*) I only hope I won't make you too miserable.

HELEN. I shan't care.

There is the sound of a key in the front door. HELEN *and* DAVID *part.*

JOAN. (*Off, in the hall.*) Damn this key! It always sticks. (*She comes in carrying a large parcel which she puts down on the table.*) Fifty, at threepence each. God bless Woolworth's! Helen, I bought you a present. (*She takes something out of her bag and hands it to* HELEN.)

HELEN. Thank you so much, Joan. It's sweet. What is it?

JOAN. You stick it in your hat, darling. David, I've bought you some shaving soap.

DAVID. I don't need any shaving soap.

JOAN. It'll come in useful later, anyway.

DAVID. Well, thanks so much.

JOAN. Not at all. Whenever I go into Woolworth's I love to buy up the whole shop. (*She picks up the parcel and goes to the door. Calling.*) Williams! (*To* HELEN *and* DAVID.) I bought John a little duck for his bath. Do you think he'll like it?

DAVID. I'm sure he'll love it.

WILLIAMS *comes in.*

JOAN. Oh, Williams. These are glasses for tonight. Take care of them, will you?

WILLIAMS. Yes, madam. (*He takes the parcel.*)

JOAN. How are things going in the dining-room?

WILLIAMS. Quite well, I think, madam.

JOAN. I'll come and help you in a minute.

WILLIAMS *goes out.* JOAN *takes off her hat and goes to the drink table.*

(*With a sigh.*) Oh, Lord, I wonder why one gives parties. (*She pours herself out a drink.*) David, I've just thought of something. Darling, I'm afraid you'll have to go down to the cellar and bring some up.

DAVID. Can't Williams do that?

JOAN. You know he can't, darling; he's far too busy. Besides, he's got this passion for 'Buy British'. If we sent him down, he'd probably bring up a couple of flagons of somebody else's glorious Emu.

DAVID. Nobody will drink wine, anyway.

JOAN. I know, darling, but it looks nice to have it, all the same.

DAVID. How much do we want?

JOAN. About a dozen bottles.

DAVID. How many pairs of hands do you think I've got?

JOAN. I'll get John to help you. Where *is* the old drunk?

HELEN. In David's room.

JOAN *goes to door of* DAVID*'s room and knocks.*

JOAN. (*Calling.*) John. Come out of there. (*To* HELEN *and* DAVID.) I'll bet he's in a delicious coma.

JOHN *opens the door.*

JOHN. I am not, nor have I been, in a coma. I've been reading Gibbon.

DAVID. I'll bet you have.

JOAN. John, you're to help David bring some bottles up from the cellar.

JOHN. But there are some stairs to go down.

JOAN. It'll do you good. It might take some of that stomach off.

JOHN. Can't David do it by himself?

JOAN. Now, don't argue. Be a good boy; and when you come back I'll give you a little present.

JOHN. Give me the present now, and I'll see if it's worth my while.

JOAN. All right – here you are. It's for your bath.

JOHN. Thank you, Joan; it's very nice.

DAVID. When John's in his bath I should have thought there wasn't much room for a foreign body.

JOAN. The keys are hanging up in the kitchen, David. I'm going next door to see how Williams is getting on.

JOAN *goes out.*

DAVID. Come on, John. Let's get this ordeal over.

JOHN. You go ahead and choose the wine. I'll follow you down in two minutes. I just want time for one little sip. I'm feeling a trifle weak.

DAVID. The effects of Gibbon, I suppose. Helen, will you see that he does come down?

HELEN. I will.

DAVID *goes out.*

JOHN *goes to the drink table.*

JOHN. May I be the first to tender my congratulations?

HELEN *wheels round and stares at him.*

HELEN. You've been listening!

JOHN. Only to parts of your conversation. Some of it was too embarrassingly sentimental, even for me.

HELEN. What a filthy trick.

JOHN. Isn't it? It's a habit I've never been able to break myself of. (*He comes back with his drink.*) You know, I'm not the least bit sincere in my congratulations. I think you're both of you making a huge mistake.

HELEN. I don't think it matters much to either David or me what you think.

JOHN. Oh no, I realise that. Still, I don't think I should ever forgive myself if I let this moment slip without uttering at least one word of warning.

HELEN. You can keep it to yourself. I'm not interested.

JOHN. (*Ignoring her.*) Now, I was at school with David, and I've known him pretty closely ever since. You, I think, have known him a month.

HELEN. That makes no difference. I know David much better than any of you.

JOHN. My dear little lamb, you're in love with him. You've so glamorised and romanticised him that as far as you're concerned he hardly exists at all outside your imagination. A romantic little girl's imagination.

HELEN. That's a lie. Let me tell you –

JOHN. (*Ignoring her.*) Now, I give you credit for enough brains to see quite clearly one side of David that most people miss. You've seen that he's got a vague desire to get away from the life he's leading now.

HELEN. That's exactly what he's going to do.

JOHN. And that's exactly where you're both making your mistake. (*With emphasis.*) He can't do it. Believe me, my dear Helen, it's quite crazy to bring that ambition of his out into the light as you're doing, because it's not a real thing at all, and when you do bring it out it'll just fade away into nothing. Just like that. (*He flicks his fingers airily.*)

HELEN. I don't believe you.

JOHN. Why should you? You're in love with him. (*He gets up and puts his empty glass back on the table*.) Well, duty calls me. I'll leave you with one more thought: David can't go back and start again because, although he wants to, he hasn't got the character to do it. Now I – I *have* got the character to do it – but then, of course, I don't want to. So there you are, you see. That's life. Ponder it, my child; it's worth pondering.

He goes out. HELEN, left alone, moves about restlessly. She takes up the script of DAVID's book, glances through it impatiently, and, on an impulse, carries it over to the writing-desk and drops it into the waste-paper basket. Then she goes to the door and opens it.

HELEN. (*Calling.*) Joan!

JOAN. (*Off.*) Yes, darling?

HELEN. (*Calling.*) Can I see you?

JOAN. (*Off.*) Darling, you're all alone. I'm so sorry. (*She comes in.*) How rude of us all.

HELEN. It wasn't that. I want to talk to you.

JOAN reacts visibly to the tone of HELEN's voice. She comes in and shuts the door.

JOAN. (*Quietly.*) Yes, Helen?

HELEN. This may be a great shock to you, but I'm afraid I can't wait for a better opportunity to talk to you. I've got to tell you now.

JOAN. Yes, Helen. What is it?

HELEN. David and I are in love with each other.

There is a pause. JOAN shows no emotion.

JOAN. Yes, I knew that.

HELEN. That makes it much easier, then. How did you know? Has David told you?

JOAN. No. But I've known he was in love with you for a little time now.

HELEN. From the time I got him to give up drinking?

JOAN. Yes, that was when I first knew. Why are you telling me now?

HELEN. Because we want to get married, Joan.

JOAN. Oh – oh, I see.

She sits down slowly.

HELEN. That means you'll have to divorce him.

JOAN. Yes. Yes, of course.

HELEN. I'm sorry, Joan. This is horrible for me, having to tell you like this.

JOAN. Why didn't David tell me?

HELEN. He wanted to, but I thought it was easier for me.

JOAN. It would be harder for him, I suppose.

Pause. JOAN *looks round the room vacantly.*

HELEN. Joan, I do hope you don't feel all this too badly.

JOAN *looks up at her.*

JOAN. My dear Helen, only this afternoon I was having a good laugh with David about this very situation.

HELEN. Then you did discuss me with him?

JOAN. As a joke, that was all. When you know something is going to happen, it makes it seem further off to joke about it.

HELEN. I'm sorry, Joan. I see you do feel this.

JOAN. One gets used to things after twelve years.

HELEN. I know. But it makes it easier, your not being in love with David, doesn't it?

JOAN. Much easier – yes.

HELEN. David told me about your marriage.

JOAN. It makes a good story, doesn't it? It's one of his best.

HELEN. He only told me that you weren't in love with each other when you got married.

JOAN. He didn't tell you about the party we gave after the wedding; how it was raided by the police, and how we made the police join in and drink our health? Or about how we woke up the next day and he said, 'Darling, I know we've forgotten something. Isn't today the day we're getting married?' Or about how – oh, hell, it goes on for ever. It's a wonderful story. It's a bit exaggerated over twelve years, but it's still very funny.

HELEN. Poor Joan!

JOAN. (*Rising.*) Helen, do you mind if we talk about this whole business some other time?

HELEN. No, of course not.

JOAN. I suppose there are lots of boring details to be discussed – about the divorce, and so on?

HELEN. We can get our lawyers to do that.

JOAN. Yes, I suppose we can. (*With an attempt at a laugh.*) Let's have a quiet little divorce, shall we, with only the family as guests.

HELEN. Thank you, Joan, for taking this so well.

JOAN. Have I taken it well? I didn't know.

HELEN. You've taken it wonderfully. (*Hesitantly.*) I want you to know that this – all this isn't going to make any difference. I mean, I know David's very fond of you, and he'd hate it if he weren't going to see you again, or anything.

JOAN. That's very kind of you.

HELEN *goes to the door.*

HELEN. Well, I must go. I do hope I haven't been too brutal about this, but I just didn't know how else to tell you, and I had to tell you now.

JOAN. You've been very – sympathetic is the word, I think.

HELEN. You're not going to hate me, are you?

JOAN. Why on earth should I hate you?

She opens the door for her, and HELEN *passes through.*

Goodbye, Helen. You're coming to this god-awful party, aren't you? I'll never forgive you if you don't.

HELEN. (*In the hall.*) Of course. I'm looking forward to it.

JOAN. Liar!

HELEN *is having difficulty in opening the door.*

Damn that lock! It always sticks. Turn it hard. Try and surprise it, if you know what I mean.

HELEN *opens the door.*

JOAN. That's right. Goodbye, Helen, see you later.

HELEN. (*In the hall.*) Goodbye, Joan, and thank you.

She goes out. JOAN *closes the door of the sitting-room. She stands, staring vacantly ahead of her for a moment, then goes over to the mirror over the fireplace right. She gazes at her reflection.* JOHN *comes in left with some bottles of wine under his arm. He puts them down on the table. He goes up to her and puts his hand on her shoulder.*

JOHN. Well, I suppose she's told you.

JOAN *nods into the mirror.*

(*Sincerely.*) I'm terribly sorry, Joan.

JOAN *turns round suddenly and buries her head in his shoulder, sobbing hysterically.* JOHN *waits for the first outburst to subside.*

You damn fool! Why didn't you *tell* her you were in love with him?

JOAN. It wouldn't have done any good.

JOHN. It was worth trying. She doesn't know.

JOAN. Besides, what's the use, if he loves her?

JOHN. I don't believe he does, really.

JOAN. Oh, yes, he does.

JOHN. He's quite mad.

JOAN. He knows what he's doing. I'm not much use to him any longer, since I've got old.

JOHN. (*After a pause.*) You should have let him know you were in love with him. That's all he wants, really – someone to be in love with him.

JOAN. Not me. He doesn't want me to be in love with him. I'd have bored him to death if I'd ever let him see it. I know that.

JOHN. It's awful how two people can misunderstand each other as much as you and David have over twelve years.

JOAN. Was I wrong, John, not to let him know?

JOHN. It was all he wanted.

JOAN. It's too late now, anyway.

JOHN. What are you going to do?

JOAN. I don't know. Oh, John, I do need him so much – so much more than Helen.

She cries again.

JOHN. You'll forget him.

There is a sound of someone in the hall. JOHN *and* JOAN *break apart.* JOAN, *with her back to the door, hastily dabs her eyes.* DAVID *comes in, carrying bottles.*

DAVID. (*Putting the bottles down on the table.*) That's nine altogether. It's got to do. Do you want them in here or in the dining-room?

JOAN. In the dining-room.

DAVID. All right. Come on, John. Bring those in.

He goes out, carrying the bottles. JOHN *goes to the table and picks up the rest.*

JOHN. Just a slave around the house, that's all I am.

He goes out, carrying the bottles.

JOAN *hastily goes to the mirror and repairs the damage to her make-up. Then she turns back and starts to walk out. The typescript of* DAVID*'s book, sticking out of the waste-paper basket, happens to catch her eye. She takes it out, and is glancing at it when* DAVID *comes back into the room.*

JOAN. David, some idiot dropped your book in the waste-paper basket.

DAVID. Oh, thanks. As a matter of fact, I'm scrapping the whole thing and starting again.

JOAN. Are you sure you're right? I think it's very good.

DAVID *shakes his head.*

You really are going to start again?

DAVID *nods.*

Well, don't throw it away. Keep it – as a sentimental memory, if nothing else. After all, it may be worthless now, but it might be pleasant to look back on later when you're an old and successful man. (*She hands him the book.*) I'm going next door. That idiot Williams has got everything all balled up in there. (*She goes to the door.*) Bring me a gin and tonic, will you, darling? And don't drown it. I want to taste the gin.

She goes out.

DAVID *puts his book in a drawer of the desk and then goes to the drink table.*

Curtain.

Act Two, Scene Two

Scene: The same. About 1 a.m. that night. The party is in full swing. All the characters so far introduced are present, with the exception of JOHN *and* PETER. *Neither the men nor the women are in evening dress. Most of them look rather untidy and dishevelled. All the guests are of roughly the same age, middle and late thirties.*

The first impression on the rise of the curtain is one of noise. Everyone is talking at once very loudly, and the gramophone is going at full strength. WILLIAMS *and an assistant are circulating among the guests replenishing drinks. Two people are just drifting out through the door left. A couple standing downstage have evidently been quarrelling; their voices rise until finally they are audible above the din. Their names are* MOYA LEXINGTON *and* LAWRENCE WALTERS.

LAWRENCE. Don't be such a silly little bore.

MOYA. I'm not being a bore. It's you who are being a bore.

LAWRENCE. I've a good mind to slap you very hard indeed.

MOYA. Go on, slap away; I'll slap back!

DAVID. Queensberry rules, please.

LAWRENCE. David, Moya's being a silly bitch.

DAVID. I'm sure she is. (*He puts his arm round her waist affectionately.*) You always are, aren't you, Moya darling?

MOYA. David, it's a heavenly party, and Joan's looking lovely, and you're my favourite man, anyhow.

LAWRENCE. Don't try to get out of it, Moya.

MOYA. All right, tell him. I'm not ashamed of it.

LAWRENCE. She said she thought the Marx Brothers were torture.

DAVID. (*Severely.*) All that flying to Australia and back has evidently turned her brain.

MOYA. David, have I told you I'm going to fly over the Pole next month?

DAVID. Yes, I read all about it in the papers.

LAWRENCE. (*Viciously.*) I suppose you think Mickey Mouse is better than Donald Duck?

MOYA. Yes, I do, as a matter of fact.

LAWRENCE. (*Helplessly.*) Oh, my God.

MOYA. Oh, look, there's Doris. I must go and find out if it's true about that taximan.

She makes her way over to the corner of the room and embraces a woman affectionately.

LAWRENCE. David, this is a heavenly party. It's like old times.

DAVID. Very old times, I'm afraid.

A WOMAN. (*Entering.*) My dear, I've just had the most horrible experience.

MOYA. (*Vaguely, to a group of people.*) Have you heard, I'm going to fly over the Pole.

A MAN. Why?

CYRIL. I think she's very bold to go over the Pole.

JOAN comes in.

JOAN. (*Shouting.*) Hi, everybody!

People stop talking and turn.

If you haven't fed already, you'd better go and do it now, otherwise there won't be anything left at all. Those pigs in there have got a good start on you.

There is a general movement towards the door. JOAN runs over to MOYA.

Moya, my angel, how are you? When did you sneak in?

People are going out of the room, still chattering.

MOYA. I've been here ages, darling. You've said 'Hello' to me twice already.

JOAN. Have I really? Isn't it awful? I'm stinking.

MOYA. It suits you, darling. You look heavenly tonight.

JOAN. I'm almost drunk enough to believe it.

MOYA. Joan, isn't it terrible? It's not true about Doris and the taximan.

JOAN. Oh, my God, and I've been dining out on that story for weeks. What a shame! Any more news, Moya?

MOYA. Nothing much. I suppose you've heard I'm flying over the Pole next week?

JOAN. (*Vaguely.*) Are you, Moya? Mind you wrap up well.

JULIA advances on JOAN, with DAVID and JOHN, and a man called ARTHUR POWER behind them. MOYA follows the others out into the supper-room.

JULIA. Here's somebody who's been trying to say 'Hello' to you all the evening.

JOAN. Arthur! My own lovely Arthur! This is my first love. How are you, Arthur? I haven't seen you for ages. What are you doing?

JULIA. My dear, haven't you heard? He's cleaning windows in Manchester. He's gone dreary on us.

JOAN. I don't believe it. He could never go dreary. He's a heavenly man. Arthur and I nearly got married once.

JULIA. It's just as well you didn't, or you'd be cleaning windows by now. You stick to David, darling. He's much more your mark.

DAVID. I don't see why it should be so dreary to clean people's windows. I should think it'd be rather gay; it might give one a new insight into human nature.

ARTHUR. Oh, I don't clean them myself, you know. I just run the business. I like it, too. That's the funny thing.

JULIA. You see. He's not at all like the old Arthur we used know.

ARTHUR. You mean the young Arthur you used to know.

JULIA. There you are, you see. He keeps on saying things like that. I tell you he's gone dreary on us. It's awful how all our old friends are going dreary on us. Either that, or they're dying. Thank God, anyway, for you and Joan. You two, anyway, will always be here.

DAVID. Suppose we go next door and get some food.

JULIA. Good idea; I'm starving.

JOHN. I've eaten two suppers already. I don't think even I could stand a third.

ARTHUR. I'm not hungry either.

JULIA. Come along, David. It's very good for one to eat at this time of night. It makes one feel much better in the morning.

   DAVID *and* JULIA *go out.*

JOAN. (*A little drunkenly.*) Don't you find it funny to think I nearly married Arthur, John?

JOHN. Not particularly.

JOAN. I think it's funny.

   She goes out. ARTHUR *and* JOHN *are now alone on the stage.*

JOHN. Well, Arthur, are you enjoying the party?

ARTHUR. I'm hating it like hell.

JOHN. Why?

ARTHUR. I think it's obscene to see a lot of middle-aged men and women behaving like children at a school treat. It's the bright young people over again, only they never were bright and now they're not even young.

JOHN. I don't think one should ever grudge people the form of escape they choose, however childish it is. I think they are very wise.

ARTHUR. It may be wise to try to escape from the world as it is at the moment, but it isn't exactly brave.

JOHN. Who wants to be brave, anyway? I'm very happy to run away from the world.

ARTHUR. Until the world catches you up by blowing you to pieces in the next war.

JOHN. Yes, or by making me trip on a banana skin in the street. I can't see much difference.

ARTHUR. The banana skin wouldn't be there if someone had picked it up first. And the next war wouldn't be there if people took the trouble to prevent it.

JOHN. I hope people do prevent it. I shall be very grateful to them.

ARTHUR. We had our chance to do it after the last war, but we all ran away instead. The awful thing is that we're still running away. I didn't realise that so much until tonight.

JOHN. You're not running away, Arthur. You're cleaning windows.

ARTHUR. Yes, I'm cleaning windows.

JOHN. I'm sure you have to face life squarely to clean windows for a living.

ARTHUR *is silent.*

It's depressing how many of the old crowd have settled down into the common rut of dreary life like you.

ARTHUR. The majority, thank God. People like you and David and Joan and the rest of this awful crowd here tonight are as dated as hell. I suppose you realise that.

JOHN. Of course we realise that. It makes it all the more fun.

ARTHUR. Don't you ever feel bored with all this?

JOHN. Only very rarely.

ARTHUR. Look here; why don't you come and work for me?

JOHN *laughs as if* ARTHUR *had made a joke.*

Seriously, why don't you?

JOHN. I'm sorry. I thought you were having your little joke.

ARTHUR. No, really, I'm serious. I need someone to help me, and I'd like to have you.

JOHN. What would you pay me?

ARTHUR. Let's say five pounds a week.

JOHN. How furious you'd be if I accepted your offer!

ARTHUR. I'd be surprised, but I'd be delighted. Of course, you realise you will have to live in Manchester, don't you?

JOHN. Obviously you're regretting your decision and are trying to put me off.

ARTHUR. It's a genuine offer. Are you going to take it?

JOHN. (*To himself.*) Five pounds a week and Manchester. (*To* ARTHUR.) No, thanks.

ARTHUR. I'll make it six pounds a week.

JOHN. But it's still Manchester. My God, I must be stinking. Cleaning windows in Manchester – me! (*Rising with dignity.*) How dare you?

ARTHUR *laughs.*

ARTHUR. The offer is open whenever you like to take it.

JOAN *comes in, laughing helplessly and hysterically. It's some seconds before she can speak.*

JOAN. Oh, John, I've got to tell you. It'll kill you. (*She laughs again.*)

JOHN. It's got to be good after this.

JOAN. I just heard Moya trying to get Lawrence to sniff a little of her 'uppies', and he said he was afraid of it being habit-forming; so she said, 'Habit-forming, my dear, what nonsense. Look at me, I've been taking it for fourteen years.' It's true. I heard her.

She doubles up with laughter again. Neither ARTHUR *nor* JOHN *joins her.* JOAN *recovers herself with difficulty.*

Damn you both for not thinking it's funny. God, I'm tired.

She sits down.

JOHN. Stay here and be quiet for a bit.

JOAN. No, I can't. I've got to keep going. (*She stares vacantly round the room.*) Phew! This room's like an oven.

She goes to the french windows at the back and throws them open, revealing a couple on the balcony clasped in a fierce embrace. They break apart.

JOAN. Oh, I'm so sorry.

THE MAN. Not at all.

JOAN. If – er – you can bear the thought of it, there's some food for you next door.

THE MAN. Thanks. That'll be delightful.

With composure he links the WOMAN*'s arm in his, and together they go out.*

JOAN. Can you beat that? Piggy Mainwaring's boy friend and that Perry girl. Oh, I just can't wait to tell Moya. It'll kill her.

She goes out.

ARTHUR. My God, how Joan has changed.

JOHN. You were really in love with her once, weren't you?

ARTHUR. Why does Joan behave like this? She used not to.

JOHN. It's become a habit, like Moya's 'uppies'.

ARTHUR. But why did she start the habit?

JOHN. To please David.

ARTHUR. I see.

JOHN. You don't, but let's leave it. (*He gets up.*) I'm going next door, in case I'm missing anything.

PETER *comes in left, wearing a hat and coat.*

Hello, Peter!

PETER. Is David in the dining-room?

JOHN. Yes, I think so.

PETER. I don't want to go in there myself. Would you mind awfully telling him I'd like to see him for a moment?

JOHN. Not at all – if I can tear him away from his guests. Are you coming, Arthur?

ARTHUR. Hell, yes, I suppose so.

JOHN *and* ARTHUR *go out. After a pause* DAVID *enters.*

DAVID. Hello! I hear you want to speak to me.

PETER. Yes, I do. I won't keep you a minute.

DAVID *comes in and shuts the door.*

I just want to tell you that I am leaving this flat tonight. I am going to stay with a friend of mine; I'm getting out tonight.

DAVID. Peter, I can't let you do that.

PETER. Don't worry; I'll be all right.

DAVID. I have to worry. Ever since your mother's death I've been more or less responsible for you. How are you going to live?

PETER. I'll get myself a decent job, and, my God, I'll be glad to get out of this flat.

DAVID. You must have some money to live on until you get a job.

PETER. You can keep your filthy money. I don't need it. I never want to see you or speak to you again as long as I live. Or Helen.

DAVID. (*After a pause.*) Peter, I'm so sorry.

PETER. (*Violently.*) Damn you! Don't be sorry for me. I'm not sorry for myself. I'm glad this has happened. I've learnt a hell of a lot. You see, I believe in a few things – things you don't believe in. Oh, I know I'm a bore – that's the word, isn't it, according to you and John – and Helen? Well, I'm still a bore, and I'm going on being a bore, and if Helen would rather lead your sort of life, well, then, I wish her luck. I can only thank God I've found out about her in time.

DAVID. (*Pause.*) Peter, aren't you being rather ungrown-up about this? I'm sure you'll get over it. I know how you feel at the moment.

PETER. Oh, do you? (*Turns and stares at him.*) Goodbye. (*He crosses to the door.*)

DAVID. Peter, where can I find you?

PETER. (*At door.*) You can't find me.

DAVID. (*Desperately.*) Peter, please don't stop me from helping you until you can find a job.

PETER *slams the door. DAVID stares at it for a second, and then turns back with a weary shrug. He takes a cigarette from a box on the table and lights it. HELEN comes in, carrying her coat.*

HELEN. I'm going, David. (*Formally, as a joke.*) Thank you for a most delightful evening. I can't tell you how much I've enjoyed myself.

DAVID. I've just been talking to Peter.

HELEN. Oh. (*She puts her coat down.*) Was it very difficult?

DAVID. There wasn't anything I could say.

HELEN. Poor David!

DAVID *turns round.*

PETER. 'Poor Peter' is what you ought to have said, isn't it?

HELEN. No. We've got to forget about Peter.

PETER. I wish to God I could. This afternoon I only thought of Peter as a vague abstract problem that could be easily solved. I didn't think of him, somehow, as an unhappy little boy.

HELEN. Shut up, David. Come and kiss me.

DAVID goes to her and kisses her.

DAVID. Helen, what have you got me into?

HELEN. Cheer up; the worst is over. We've told them both, and one of them, anyway, has taken it marvellously.

DAVID. (*With an attempt at a smile.*) She's taken it a bit too marvellously. I'm rather hurt.

HELEN. You haven't talked to her yet, have you?

DAVID. I haven't had a chance. She's been so busy being the life and soul of the party, I haven't been able to get near her.

HELEN. You'll stay friends with her, won't you, David, after we're married?

DAVID. Of course I will. I couldn't bear it if I was never going to see her again. But it's not Joan I'm worrying about.

HELEN. (*Warningly.*) Darling, I've told you you're not to think about Peter.

DAVID is silent, evidently not taking her advice. He turns away from her.

(*Sharply.*) David, come here.

DAVID goes to her again, smiles, and kisses her. JOAN comes in and stands at the door, watching them. She is turning to go out when HELEN sees her.

HELEN. Hello, Joan! (*She releases DAVID quite casually.*) I was just going to find you to tell you how much I enjoyed your party.

JOAN. You're not going already? The party's hardly started.

HELEN. I must, really. (*She looks at her watch.*) Heavens! Half-past one.

JOAN. (*Wearily.*) Is it only that? I thought it was much later.

HELEN. That's quite late enough for me. Goodbye Joan. Thanks so much.

JOAN. Goodbye, Helen.

They shake hands.

HELEN. I'll come and see you tomorrow, if I may.

JOAN. (*Vaguely.*) Tomorrow?

HELEN. Or are you doing something?

JOAN. No, I'm not doing anything tomorrow.

HELEN. I'll come in some time in the afternoon, then. I know you'll want to sleep late. Goodbye, David.

DAVID. Goodbye, Helen.

She goes out. JOAN *looks at* DAVID, *then turns away quickly. She picks up some empty glasses, takes them over to a tray in the corner without speaking.* DAVID *is silent, too. He is plainly embarrassed.*

JOAN. (*At length.*) She's a nice girl. I'm sure you will be happy with her.

DAVID. I'm glad you don't mind too much about it.

JOAN *mechanically collects some more empty glasses, and* DAVID *continues.*

You don't, do you?

JOAN. It was bound to happen sooner or later.

DAVID. I'm sorry it should have happened at all.

JOAN. You don't mean that – so you shouldn't say it.

DAVID. I only mean that we've had such a lovely time together for so long, it seems idiotic to break it all now.

JOAN. Twelve years and seven months. We didn't think it would last as long as that when we got married, did we?

DAVID. (*Smiling.*) Speak for yourself. I hoped it was going to last a lifetime.

JOAN. Did you, David?

DAVID. Didn't you?

JOAN. There's a difference between hoping and thinking.

DAVID. I'm glad in a way we didn't make the mistake of falling in love with each other. I sometimes wonder if ours isn't perhaps the best basis of all for marriage.

JOAN. Perhaps it is.

DAVID. It's worked very well with us, hasn't it?

JOAN. It might have worked even better if we'd been in love with each other, like you and Helen.

DAVID. That's a different thing altogether. I don't even know if I like Helen as a person – in the way I like you. I only know I love her, and that's something you can't explain.

JOAN. You didn't want to fall in love with Helen, did you?

DAVID. I tried hard enough not to.

JOAN. It's hell that, isn't it – trying to stop yourself falling in love?

DAVID. It can't be done, I'm afraid.

JOAN. If it could, life would be a lot easier. I'm going to have another drink. What about you?

DAVID. No, thanks.

JOAN. Of course, I was forgetting. (*She pours herself a drink.*) You know, David, I could have helped you to give up drinking if only I'd known you really wanted to.

DAVID. I didn't want to. I'd have died of cirrhosis if I'd gone on, that's all.

JOAN. Oh, you didn't tell me that.

DAVID. It was all rather boring. There wasn't any need to bother you with it all.

JOAN. I'm afraid I haven't been a very good wife.

DAVID. (*Smiling.*) But you've been a marvellous wife.

JOAN. You see, I've made a silly mistake about you. I thought you really were bored with people like – like Helen, and with the idea of not drinking, and leading a serious life and all that. If only I'd known I might have been able to help you perhaps a little bit more with your work and – and things. Like Helen is doing now. Only, of course, I could never have done it as well.

DAVID. I suppose I was ashamed to show you that side of myself. Anyway, I wouldn't have bored you with all that.

JOAN. It's silly, isn't it? I wouldn't have been bored at all.

There is a raucous shout of laughter from the next room.

I suppose we ought to go and break that party in there.

DAVID. I'll go and bring them in. You sit down and rest. You must be dead tired.

He goes to the door.

JOAN. No, don't go. (*He stops.*) Play something. Do you mind? They'll come back in here when they hear that.

DAVID. It'd be easier –

JOAN. Do play something.

DAVID. (*Goes to the piano.*) All right. What?

JOAN. 'Avalon'. Do you mind?

DAVID. I've almost forgotten it. I'll try. (*He plays the tune.*)

JOAN *comes behind the piano.*

I used to love this tune.

JOAN. I still do.

DAVID. I'm afraid I'm not playing it very well.

JOAN. You never did play it very well.

*He continues to play it for a moment, humming the tune gently.
JOAN kisses the top of his head. He reaches up and takes her
hand.*

Go on playing.

DAVID *drops her hand and continues to play.* JOHN *comes in
silently and watches the two.* JOAN *goes quietly to french
windows at the back.*

JOAN. Go on playing this for a bit, David. Do you mind?

DAVID *nods.* JOAN *steps on to the balcony and pulls the
curtains shut behind her.*

DAVID. Well, John, I hear you know all about it.

JOHN. All about it, yes.

DAVID. You think I'm a damn fool, don't you?

JOHN. Much worse than that.

He lies down on the sofa. DAVID *continues playing. People
start to drift in from the dining-room.*

MOYA. Heavenly tune, this. I came out to it.

JULIA. It's agony to hear it again, isn't it?

MOYA. Exquisite agony.

JULIA. Who was that divine man who used to sing it?

MOYA. My dear, he went to Australia.

JULIA. How awful!

*About ten people group themselves around the piano and start
to sing drunkenly and sentimentally.*

JOHN *rises, goes out to balcony and returns, pulling the
curtains wide open. The balcony is seen to be empty. He tries
to attract* DAVID*'s attention.* DAVID *and the rest go on
singing.*

Curtain.

Act Three

Scene: the same. About three months later. Late afternoon.

MISS POTTER, *a severe-looking woman of about forty, wearing horn-rimmed glasses, is sitting in an armchair, knitting.* JOHN *is at the bookcase, pulling down books, glancing at the fly-leaves and either putting them on the table or replacing them in the bookcase.*

JOHN. There are two or three of these novels I don't want, Miss Potter, if you care to have them.

MISS POTTER. It's very kind of you, Mr Reid, but I think you'd better give them to someone else. You see, I very rarely read novels.

JOHN. What do you do with yourself all day long, then?

MISS POTTER. When I'm not working, I like to knit.

JOHN. I should imagine you'll be doing quite a lot of knitting in the near future, then.

MISS POTTER. You mean I shall be doing very little work in the near future?

JOHN. (*Looking at her distastefully.*) That was what I intended to imply.

MISS POTTER. I hope you are right.

JOHN. You haven't any objection to not working?

MISS POTTER. Who has?

JOHN. Your predecessor had.

MISS POTTER. Then she was a fool.

JOHN. It wasn't a she. It was a he, and a young he, too, which explains it.

WILLIAMS *comes in with an armful of socks, handkerchiefs and shirts.*

Oh, Williams, I've put the books I want packed on the table.

WILLIAMS. Yes, sir.

JOHN. What are those things you've got there?

WILLIAMS. They came from your drawer sir. Six handkerchiefs, four pairs of socks and three shirts.

JOHN. Well?

WILLIAMS. They're marked with Mr Scott-Fowler's name, sir. I was wondering whether I shouldn't return them to him.

JOHN. Well, stop wondering and go back and pack them.

WILLIAMS. (*Doubtfully.*) Suppose Mr Scott-Fowler notices they've gone, sir?

JOHN. Then I'll send them back. But he won't notice; don't worry. He owes me a parting gift, anyway.

WILLIAMS. Yes, sir.

JOHN. How are things going?

WILLIAMS. Quite well, I think sir. I have packed practically everything.

JOHN. (*Looks at his watch.*) Call me a taxi in about half an hour, will you?

WILLIAMS. Yes, sir.

He goes out.

JOHN *goes to the window and looks out.*

JOHN. Spring's been in the air today, Miss Potter. Does that thrill you?

MISS POTTER. Not at all. It's a most over-rated season, I think. I don't like green as a colour, and I hate bird-noises.

JOHN. Doesn't it fill you with the joy of being alive, or something, as it's supposed to?

MISS POTTER. It gives me a cold and makes my teeth ache usually.

JOHN. It does with me, too, but I still like it. (*He gazes out of the window.*) I'm told the sun never shines in Manchester.

MISS POTTER. That's nonsense. It does, quite often. It's not the Riviera, of course, but when the sun does shine in Manchester you'll find you'll appreciate it all the more.

JOHN. That's encouraging to know. Is it as dirty a town as they say it is?

MISS POTTER. I'd hardly know about that. When I was there I was only a child, you see.

JOHN. You misunderstand me, Miss Potter. I'm not asking you about the red light district. I only want to know if it's true you have to take three baths a day up there to keep even vaguely clean.

MISS POTTER. There's a certain amount of soot in the atmosphere, of course, but it only makes your hands and face dirty. Three baths a day is an exaggeration.

JOHN. Shall I turn back before it's too late, Miss Potter?

MISS POTTER. Of course not. You'll enjoy it. It's not a very beautiful city, I'll admit, but the people are friendly and charming: Hail-fellow-well-met, if you know what I mean.

JOHN. Oh God, how well I know what you mean! Please don't talk about Manchester any more, Miss Potter. With every word you say my resolve is fading.

HELEN *comes in and advances on* JOHN *with a friendly smile.*

HELEN. Well, John, I just came in to say goodbye and wish you good luck. Good afternoon, Miss Potter.

MISS POTTER. Good afternoon.

JOHN. Thanks, Helen.

They shake hands.

HELEN. How do you feel? A bit frightened, I should think, aren't you?

JOHN. Not frightened. In the depths of despair, that's all; thanks to Miss Potter's vivid little word pictures of Manchester.

HELEN. It's one of the greatest miracles of the age. I still can't believe it.

JOHN. (*Gloomily.*) Nor can I.

HELEN. It all happened so suddenly. David only told me about it the other day. When did you decide to go?

JOHN. When Arthur first offered me the job. But it took me three months to decide to act on my decision.

HELEN. I bet you'll be back in a week.

JOHN. No, I'm never coming back. I'm going to my grave – a sooty, hail-fellow-well-met grave. Will you excuse me, Helen; I've got to superintend packing.

He goes out.

HELEN. He doesn't seem to like your description of Manchester, Miss Potter.

MISS POTTER. It's just as well he should be depressed now. Then he won't be so depressed when he gets there.

HELEN *laughs and takes a cigarette from a box with a proprietary air.*

HELEN. Where's Mr Scott-Fowler?

MISS POTTER. He's in his room, I believe.

HELEN. Working?

MISS POTTER. I've no idea.

HELEN *picks up a book from two or three on the table.*

HELEN. I see you've got those books from the London Library.

MISS POTTER. Yes, I went out to get them yesterday.

HELEN *picks them up one by one.*

HELEN. (*Reading the titles.*) 'Talleyrand', by Duff-Cooper; 'The Life and Times of Talleyrand'; 'Talleyrand's Memoirs'.

MISS POTTER. They're all the books the head librarian recommended.

HELEN. Did he do any work on them last night?

MISS POTTER. No, he did *The Times* crossword puzzle. I helped him.

HELEN. He promised me he'd do some work last night. That's why I specially didn't come round.

MISS POTTER. I expect he'll start tonight.

HELEN. You must be getting bored here after a week with no work to do.

MISS POTTER. Not at all. I'm perfectly happy doing nothing.

HELEN. I hoped that engaging you would make him start working again.

MISS POTTER. Don't you think perhaps it's a little too soon after his wife's death for him to concentrate on work?

HELEN. Is that the reason he gave you for not working?

MISS POTTER. He's never mentioned his wife to me. But, naturally, I read about the accident in the papers, and I can well imagine it must have been a terrible shock for him.

HELEN. Of course it was a shock for him. It was a shock for all of us; but it's nearly three months ago now, and if he started to do some work it would help him to take his mind off the whole business.

MISS POTTER. (*Curious.*) Were you at the party that night?

HELEN. Yes, but I'd left before it happened.

MISS POTTER. I went out on the balcony one night and sat on the parapet, just as she must have done. It's very easy to imagine how it could have happened. If you lean back a little too far and then look down suddenly, it would be the easiest thing in the world to lose your balance, especially as she – er – wasn't feeling too well.

HELEN. How do you mean, she wasn't feeling too well?

MISS POTTER. Well, that's just a way of saying what they said openly at the inquest – that she'd had a couple of drinks too many. Did you notice that, by the way, when you were there that night?

HELEN. (*Coldly.*) I think it would be a good thing if we all tried to forget about that night.

DAVID comes in from his room. He wears his usual tweed coat and flannel trousers, and has on a black tie. He carries a book in his hand.

DAVID. Hello, Helen, I didn't know you were here. Why didn't you let me know?

HELEN. I thought perhaps you were working, and I didn't want to disturb you.

DAVID. I couldn't have been working less.

He drops the book on the sofa. HELEN *picks it up.*

HELEN. (*Reading the title.*) 'Death in the Albert Hall'.

DAVID. It's not very good; but if you like, you can have it.

HELEN. No, thank you.

DAVID sits down.

MISS POTTER. Will you be needing me this afternooon, Mr Scott-Fowler?

DAVID. No, Miss Potter.

MISS POTTER. I think I'll go to my room and write some letters, then. (*She goes to the door.*) Would it be possible for me to have my tea in there?

DAVID. Certainly, have it in your bedroom, Miss Potter. Have it anywhere you like.

MISS POTTER. Thank you.

She goes out.

DAVID. That reminds me, I want my tea. I don't know what I'd do without it. I've become quite an addict. It can't give you cirrhosis, can it? I drink about ten cups a day.

HELEN. (*Laughs.*) You know, David, I do admire you for the way you've kept on the wagon.

DAVID. I rather admire myself for that. Though actually it hasn't been nearly as difficult as I thought it would be, thanks to you.

HELEN. You never feel you want a drink now, do you?

DAVID. I took a sniff at some whisky the other day, and believe it or not, I nearly threw up on the spot. Isn't that funny?

He holds out his hands to HELEN. HELEN *goes and kisses him and then sits on the sofa beside him.*

You pour out, darling. I never expected to see you this afternoon. It's quite a thrill.

HELEN. I thought I had to come in to say goodbye to John. Poor old thing; he's terribly depressed by it all.

DAVID. So am I. I hate the thought of his going.

HELEN. You didn't try and put him off, did you?

DAVID. Certainly I did. I argued with him for hours to stop him going.

HELEN. Oh, David, you shouldn't have done that. After all, he's doing a good thing. It was very selfish of you.

DAVID. But I am selfish. You know that.

HELEN. Yes, you are.

DAVID. So are you, darling. So don't look so pleased with yourself.

HELEN. I'm only selfish about you, not about anything else. (*She squeezes his hand.*) You know, David, I used to hate John, but now I rather like him. Funny, isn't it? (*Thoughtfully.*) He was very fond of Joan, wasn't he? Her death must have made a difference to him, too.

DAVID *withdraws his hand from hers and moves a little away.*

DAVID. (*In a different voice.*) Yes, I suppose so.

HELEN. You still can't bear me to talk about Joan, can you?

DAVID. I hate to be reminded of it, that's all.

HELEN. Darling, you've got to make up your mind that you're going to be reminded of it all your life. You're going to save yourself a lot of unpleasantness in the future if you could learn now to talk about Joan without being hurt.

DAVID. You've got a streak of hardness in you that I haven't got.

HELEN. It's not hardness. It's honesty.

DAVID. Call it that if you like. I still haven't got it.

HELEN. You should have.

DAVID *looks away from her.* HELEN *catches hold of his sleeve.*

Sorry, David.

DAVID. That's all right. I'm sorry, too. (*Pause.*) Did you see that boy yesterday – that friend of Peter's?

HELEN. Yes, I saw him, but it wasn't any good. He's looking for Peter himself.

DAVID. He must have left London.

HELEN. He may have. I've rung up all the people in town he might possibly be staying with.

DAVID. What a damn little fool he is!

HELEN. (*Quietly.*) Don't say that, David.

DAVID. I see it's my turn to suggest a change of subject.

HELEN. I know what I've got to tell you. I went to the agency yesterday. David, they've got just the cottage we want.

DAVID. Cottage?

HELEN. Well, call it a house, if you like. It's got four bedrooms, and quite a good bathroom; a big room downstairs, which we'll make into a sitting-room and dining-room in one; a little room at the back that I can turn into a study for you; five acres. All by itself in the New Forest.

DAVID. Electric light?

HELEN. (*Cheerfully.*) No.

DAVID. Water laid on?

HELEN. No. We can get the gardener to pump it up every morning.

DAVID. I know those damn things. Only a man who's stone deaf could sleep through the din they make.

HELEN. That's fine. It'll get you up early.

DAVID. The New Forest is a long way from London.

HELEN. All the better.

DAVID *gets up.*

DAVID. You didn't do anything about it, did you?

HELEN. I took an option on it.

DAVID. When for?

HELEN. Immediate occupancy. You seem a little doubtful. What's the matter?

DAVID. Darling, you know how keen I am for us to get married as soon as possible, but –

HELEN. But – ?

DAVID. Isn't it still a little soon after Joan's death? You know the sort of things people would say.

HELEN. I don't think we need care what people say.

DAVID. It's stupid, but I do care, I'm afraid. Not so much for ourselves, but for Joan's sake. Honestly I really believe it would be better if we left it a little longer.

HELEN. It's only that I hate waiting.

DAVID. Don't you think I do, too?

HELEN. I hope so.

DAVID. What do you mean, hope? You know damned well I couldn't live a day without you.

He kisses her. After a pause, still holding her in his arms.

Are you coming round tonight, or shall we go out somewhere?

HELEN. I'm leaving you alone tonight, so you can get started on those. (*She points to the London Library books.*)

DAVID. You're not leaving me alone tonight?

HELEN. Yes, I am. I'm not going to have you using me as an excuse for not working.

DAVID. I don't need any excuse for not working. If you leave me alone tonight I shall do a crossword puzzle with Miss Potter, as I did last night.

HELEN. Oh, David, I'd be so much happier if you'd keep your promise to me, and really start to do some work.

DAVID. There'll be plenty of time to study M. Talleyrand when I'm in that horrible little cottage. What's it called, by the way?

HELEN. Rose Cottage.

DAVID. I feared as much. Let's change it to Honeysuckle House shall we? And keep the roses to go round the door. Where shall we have dinner tonight? Joseph's?

HELEN. We're not having dinner, David, I've told you –

DAVID. I'll meet you at Joseph's at half-past seven. Then we can go and see Garbo, if we want to.

HELEN. All right, damn you.

DAVID. I'll bring Miss Potter along, shall I, so that if I've any brilliant thoughts about Talleyrand at dinner she can take them down.

HELEN. *I'll* take them down. I'm getting quite jealous of Miss Potter. She has a peculiar gleam in her eye when she looks at you.

DAVID. Oh, by the way, Moya's giving a party this evening. She's asked us both. What do you think? Shall we look in there before dinner? It might be quite fun.

HELEN. (*Reproachfully.*) Oh, David!

DAVID. What's the matter?

HELEN. You know what I think of Miss Moya Lexington.

DAVID. Nothing to what I think of her. Still, her parties are usually quite gay.

HELEN. You can go if you like, but I promise you nothing on earth will get me there.

DAVID. Oh, all right.

HELEN. (*After a slight pause.*) Am I being a bore, David?

DAVID. Not in the least. I quite understand. You don't want to go to Moya's party – so we won't go to Moya's party.

HELEN. Why don't you go by yourself?

DAVID. I might. I'll see how I feel.

HELEN. I'd rather you didn't.

DAVID. Then why suggest it?

HELEN. I suppose I was being unselfish. Honestly, I'd rather you didn't have anything more to do with that crowd.

DAVID. You can't touch pitch without being defiled, eh?

HELEN. Don't be silly, David.

DAVID. That's what you meant, though, wasn't it?

HELEN. You know perfectly well what I meant.

DAVID. Let's drop the subject, shall we?

HELEN. Are you going to the party?

DAVID. (*Loudly.*) No, if you feel so strongly about it. The whole thing seems to me supremely unimportant, anyway.

HELEN. Does it, David? It seems to me rather important.

There is a knock on the door.

DAVID. (*Sharply.*) Come in.

PETER *comes in. He is wearing a very shabby overcoat.*

HELEN. Peter!

PETER. I let myself in with my key. I hope you don't mind.

He is careful not to look at either HELEN *or* DAVID. HELEN *runs up to him.*

HELEN. Oh, Peter, you are a little fool. Where on earth have you been hiding yourself?

PETER. (*Not looking at her.*) I stayed with Pat Morris for a bit, and then I got some digs in Hammersmith.

DAVID. I'm awfully glad to see you, Peter.

He puts his hand out, but PETER *ignores it.*

PETER. Hello, David.

HELEN. Pat Morris, of all people! I thought of everyone else, but not of him. How are you, Peter? Are you well? Have you been all right?

PETER. Yes, thank you.

HELEN. I don't believe you've been eating enough. You look half-starved.

PETER. I'm all right.

DAVID. Why don't you sit down? Have some tea or something?

PETER. No, thank you. I can't stay long. I want to talk to you alone.

DAVID. Can't Helen . . . ?

PETER. I'd rather not.

HELEN. That's all right. I'll go. (*She gathers up her things and turns to* PETER.) I should be very angry with you, Peter. You don't know what a time I've had running all over London, looking for you.

PETER. I don't see why you should have worried about me.

HELEN. Don't you?

She smiles at him.

Really there wasn't any need to run away, you know.

PETER *still does not look at her.*

HELEN. Let's meet tomorrow, shall we? What about lunch? (*Continuing before he can answer.*) Come and pick me up at my house about one. I've got lots to talk to you about. Tell me about Pat Morris. Is he still as red as ever?

PETER. Well, he's pretty violent about things at the moment.

HELEN. I don't blame him. Has he converted you, Peter, or are you still just mildly pink?

PETER. I don't know. I don't think I'm anything at all.

HELEN. But you must be something just at this moment. You can't just stand back and watch the bombs drop.

DAVID. (*Surlily.*) Let's postpone the political discussion, shall we? I think Peter wants to talk to me.

HELEN. Yes. I must go. Goodbye, Peter. Remember our date tomorrow – and don't run away again, will you? Goodbye, David.

> HELEN *goes out. There is a pause.* PETER, *with deliberate unconcern, takes up a cigarette box, his hand shaking slightly.*

PETER. May I?

DAVID. Please do.

> PETER *lights a cigarette.*

PETER. That little scene was rather impressive. One might almost have thought she was glad to see me.

DAVID. She is glad to see you.

PETER. Why? Is she getting tired of you?

DAVID. (*Quietly.*) What did you want to say to me, Peter?

PETER. (*Turning his back.*) I want some money.

DAVID. Oh! Is that why you came back?

PETER. You didn't think this was a social call, did you?

DAVID. (*Diffidently.*) I hoped perhaps you might have forgiven me now – after all this time.

PETER. After all this time? What is it – three months? Anyway, I've got nothing to forgive.

DAVID. I'm sorry. I hoped it might be different.

> PETER *does not answer. He puts his cigarette out and faces* DAVID.

Can you let me have twenty pounds? I owe most of it in rent, and I've got to have something to live on.

DAVID. Of course. But sit down, Peter, please, and let's have a talk –

PETER. I'm sorry. I've got to go. Can I have it now, please?

DAVID. All right. (*He takes a cheque book from his pocket and goes to writing-desk.*) Are you sure that's enough?

PETER. For the moment, yes.

DAVID. By the way, I know a man in the Exchange Telegraph who says they want young men who can type and don't mind night work. I thought of you, but of course I couldn't get in touch with you. (*He hands him a cheque.*)

PETER. How much do they pay?

DAVID. Practically nothing at all to start with, I think, but apparently it's a job which can lead to something quite good in the future.

PETER. (*With a quick laugh.*) The future! That's a nice little prospect, isn't it?

DAVID. I know. It's rather hard to look ahead these days, isn't it? Still, I don't think it's worth giving up a good job just because one's afraid of what's going to happen.

PETER. That sentiment comes a little strangely from you, if you don't mind my saying so.

DAVID. I suppose it does, but somehow – about you – I mean it.

PETER. Thank you, but I don't think I'll take that job all the same.

DAVID. Have you anything else in mind?

PETER. No.

DAVID. What are you going to do then?

PETER. I don't know. It doesn't seem to matter.

DAVID *stares at* PETER. WILLIAMS *comes in.* PETER *turns his back on him.*

WILLIAMS. Mrs Browne is here, sir.

DAVID. (*Impatiently.*) I can't see anyone now.

WILLIAMS. She says she's on her way to Miss Lexington's party and just looked in to say goodbye to Mr Reid.

DAVID. Well, show her into Mr Reid's room then. He's packing.

WILLIAMS. Very good, sir.

WILLIAMS *goes out.*

DAVID. What's happened to you, Peter?

PETER. I've grown up a bit, that's all. You told me to grow up the last time I saw you. Do you remember?

DAVID. Did I?

PETER. You said I was being ungrown-up about you and Helen. You said I'd soon get over it.

DAVID. I'm sorry. It was a stupid thing to say. I didn't realise then what she meant to you.

PETER. Do you now?

DAVID. Yes, I do – now.

PETER. I don't believe it. You've never had any real feeling for anybody in your life. You don't know what it is to need somebody.

DAVID. Yes, I do.

PETER. Anyway – what the hell! I'm not crying about it. Possibly you're right. I may get over it one day.

DAVID is silent. A pause.

Well, goodbye. Thanks for this.

He puts the cheque in his pocket and goes to the door, turns, speaking very diffidently.

I'm sorry about Joan, David.

DAVID. Thank you, Peter.

PETER. I liked her awfully. It must have been a frightful shock for you.

DAVID. Yes, it was. Thank you for your letter.

PETER. That's all right. Goodbye.

He turns to go. DAVID stops him.

DAVID. Peter, listen. I'm not being a hypocrite. I know what you think of me, and I don't blame you in some ways. But I do mean this. I nearly made a mess of my life. For God's sake don't make a mess of yours.

A pause.

PETER. Do you know, I prefer the old David Scott-Fowler to the new one. I never thought you'd become a bore.

DAVID is silent, turning hopelessly away. JULIA comes in.

JULIA. David, that dirty old brute's packing all your shirts. I think he ought to be stopped. Why, Peter, of all people! How are you, angel-face? Where have you been hiding yourself all these months?

PETER. Oh, I've been – away. I'm just going. Goodbye.

He moves to the door.

JULIA. Where are you going? Anywhere in particular?

PETER. Hammersmith.

JULIA. (*With a shriek.*) Hammersmith! So that's why you've got your country tweeds on. I tell you what – why don't you come to Moya's party with me? I know she'd love to see you.

PETER. A party?

JULIA. Yes, darling. If you just wait one second while I have a drink, I'll take you along with me.

PETER. All right. Thank you very much.

JULIA. Good. (*To* DAVID). A little brandy, please, darling.

DAVID. Peter, you don't want to go to that party, do you?

PETER. Why not?

DAVID *turns abruptly to the drink table.*

DAVID (*To* JULIA.) How much soda?

JULIA. Not too much, ducky. That's enough. (*To* PETER.) Peter, my angel, how are you? Isn't it funny your hiding yourself away all this time and never coming near us. I suppose you wouldn't have heard the frightful news about Cyril. My dear, I can hardly bear to speak about it. I've been absolutely shattered.

PETER. Why? Is he dead?

JULIA. My dear, as good as. He's been conscripted. Isn't it terrible? He's being awfully brave about it, poor lamb, and so am I, but of course it's been the most terrible time for us all, as you can imagine.

PETER. Yes, of course, it would be.

JULIA. Well, David, my angel, how are you?

DAVID. All right, thank you.

JULIA. I haven't been in to see you for an awful long time, have I? As a matter of fact, I've got to admit I hate coming to this flat at all. It gives me the shudders every time I look at that balcony.

She takes her drink and wanders over to the balcony. She looks at it for a moment, and then turns with a shudder.

JULIA. Poor Joan! Life isn't the same without her. She was such fun. (*She takes a meditative sip of her brandy.*)

DAVID. Shut up, Julia. Do you mind?

JULIA. I know just how you feel about it, ducky. We all do.

Anyway, there's one consolation, isn't there – she couldn't have known anything about it for a second. It must have been just like that party years ago when Johnny Benson fell over the balustrade –

DAVID. Shut up, Julia – do you hear? Shut up.

JULIA. Oh, my dear, I'm so sorry. I wouldn't upset you for the world.

She finishes her drink.

Well, we'd better be going, Peter. Goodbye, darling. You're coming to Moya's, aren't you?

DAVID. No.

JULIA. No? I think you should. It's going to be a good party. Peter, you're not twenty, are you?

PETER. No. I'm twenty-two.

JULIA. Thank God for that.

DAVID. Peter, don't go yet. I want to talk to you.

PETER. I think we've said everything there is to say, haven't we? Goodbye.

PETER *goes out into the hall and opens the front door for* JULIA.

JULIA (*To* PETER.) Moya thought of making this a gas-mask party you know, but then she realised no one would be able to drink. So what sort of party it's going to be I don't know.

They go out. DAVID *sits on the sofa and picks up a paper, then he throws it away and begins to pace the room.* JOHN *comes in and goes over to the drink table.*

DAVID. Peter's just been here.

Pause. JOHN *sits up sharply.*

JOHN. Is all forgiven and forgotten, then?

DAVID. No. He only came round for some money to pay his rent or something.

JOHN. (*Thoughtfully.*) Poor little Peter. How he must have hated doing that.

DAVID. He's changed, John. He seems to have lost all the drive and enthusiasm he used to have.

JOHN. I'm delighted to hear it.

DAVID. He was quite apathetic just now. He doesn't even seem to hate me any more.

JOHN. Apathy is another word for contentment. Peter's lucky if he can achieve it without this.

He holds up his glass.

DAVID. He turned down a job, too.

JOHN. Did he, now? I always knew there was good in that boy.

DAVID. Cut the wisecracks, John. I'm worried.

JOHN. Why?

DAVID. I don't want him to make a mess of his life.

JOHN. Did you tell him so?

DAVID. Yes.

JOHN. That was tactful, I must say.

DAVID. I'm his guardian.

JOHN. That makes it worse, if anything. If I were your guardian, it wouldn't give me the right to hit you hard on the head with a bottle, and then reprove you sternly for looking dazed.

DAVID. Meaning I'm responsible?

JOHN. Well, aren't you?

DAVID. I suppose I am, but I don't see what the hell I'm to do about it.

JOHN. Do you really want to do something about it?

DAVID. Yes, of course.

JOHN. Well, then, it shouldn't be difficult.

DAVID. Why? What can I do?

JOHN. Do you really want me to tell you?

DAVID. Certainly.

JOHN. Give up Helen.

DAVID. I told you to drop the wisecracks.

JOHN. The awful thing about being a wisecracker is that when you say something serious, people still think it's a wisecrack.

DAVID. You couldn't have meant that seriously?

JOHN. Certainly I did. It seems to me, after due consideration, the only possible solution.

DAVID. In other words, you mean there isn't anything I can do at all?

JOHN. Yes, there is. I've told you. You can give up Helen.

DAVID. I don't want to be too rude to you, John, because you're leaving in a few minutes. But has it by any chance escaped your notice that Helen and I happen to be in love with each other?

JOHN. Yes, I have noticed that.

DAVID. Then do you really think I'm crazy enough to make that kind of sacrifice for Peter or anyone in the world? Or that Helen is either?

JOHN. Helen needn't be consulted. You could just fade away into the distance, romantically, like Sydney Carton.

DAVID. May I remind you that Sydney Carton killed himself.

JOHN. The idea is yours for what it's worth.

DAVID. (*Laughs.*) You're not drunk, are you?

JOHN. Not yet. No.

DAVID. Are you really putting forward my giving up Helen as a serious suggestion?

JOHN. A perfectly serious suggestion.

DAVID. Listen, John. If you were being slowly tortured to death before my eyes and I knew I could stop it by giving up Helen, I wouldn't do it. There isn't anybody in the world I'd make that sort of sacrifice for.

JOHN. Not even for Helen?

DAVID. What?

JOHN. I said, wouldn't you make that sacrifice even for Helen?

DAVID. If you're not drunk, you're mad.

JOHN. I think, if you won't give up Helen for Peter's sake, you should give her up for her own sake. Of course, I admit it's nothing to do with me.

He gets up and replaces his glass on the tray. DAVID *watches him, bewildered.*

DAVID. Are you trying to tell me that Helen isn't in love with me?

JOHN. No, I'm not. She's in love with you all right, and you're in love with her. The only difference between you is that in a year's time she'll be even more in love with you than she is now, and you'll undoubtedly hate her like hell.

DAVID. (*Controlling himself.*) What makes you think that?

JOHN. The fact that you half hate her already. I've watched you this last month.

DAVID. Our quarrels don't mean anything.

JOHN. They mean this much. They mean that you've already started to resent her managing your life.

DAVID. It's an effort to change my life. It's like giving up drinking. It makes one peevish and nervy. But I want to do it, and I need her help, even though I seem to resent it sometimes.

JOHN. David, you're not talking to Helen now. You don't have to put that act on with me.

DAVID. It's not an act.

JOHN. You know damn well it's an act. Look at yourself clearly for a second, will you. Honestly and truthfully tell me, do you see a man who's going to be happy living in the country with an earnest schoolgirl, sitting on his head, forcing him to work ten hours a day?

DAVID. Yes, I do.

JOHN *smiles, shrugs his shoulders.*

I admit I may fail, but there's no harm in trying, anyway.

JOHN. No harm to you, I suppose. Just a few boring weeks in a cottage. You'll soon forget that when you get back to London and start to lead your old life again.

DAVID. You think I'm too weak to go through with it?

JOHN. My dear David, I don't think: I know you are.

DAVID. Supposing I am too weak; supposing I do give up – then Helen will have to adapt herself to my life. At least I'll have tried to adapt myself to hers.

JOHN. Yes, you'll have tried, and Helen will try – and you'll kill her as surely as you killed Joan.

DAVID. (*Shouting hysterically.*) Damn you! God damn you!

JOHN. Then you know who killed her?

DAVID. (*More quietly.*) Get out! Get out of here!

Long pause. JOHN *does not move.* DAVID *sits down slowly.*

JOHN. You run away from everything, don't you? You've known for six months that Joan killed herself because of you, and you've never dared to face it.

DAVID. She couldn't have cared that much.

JOHN. She did.

DAVID. She didn't have to kill herself.

JOHN. It was just about the only thing she could do.

DAVID. Why in God's name didn't she tell me?

JOHN. She thought you'd be bored with her if you knew. To prevent herself boring you, she changed in twelve years from a rather simple little girl into what she was when she died. Her life was a fake, a performance given for your benefit.

DAVID. I must have been mad not to see it.

JOHN. No, just so utterly self-centred that nobody's feelings in the world interest you, except your own.

DAVID. (*After a pause.*) You think I might do the same to Helen?

JOHN. I think it's very possible.

DAVID. But Helen's so different from Joan.

JOHN. Not so very different from what Joan was twelve years ago. Not quite so nice, perhaps, and certainly stronger, but not so very different.

DAVID. You were in love with Joan, weren't you?

JOHN. I suppose I was.

DAVID. Why couldn't *you* do anything to help her?

JOHN. What could I have done? It was you she was in love with.

DAVID. You could have told me the truth.

JOHN. How would that have helped Joan?

DAVID *gets up and goes slowly to the window.*

DAVID. You're right about me, John. I'm entirely selfish. And that's exactly why I can't give up Helen now.

JOHN. I never expected you would. You asked my advice, and I gave it to you. That's all.

DAVID. Everything you've said may be right. It may be the same with Helen. I don't know. But I need her, and that's enough.

JOHN. Peter needs her, too, and Helen really and honestly – needs Peter.

DAVID. (*Savagely.*) What the hell is that to me?

JOHN. Nothing, of course. It's nothing to me either. I think both of them are bores, and both probably deserve what they get. (*He looks at his watch.*) I wonder if Williams has got that taxi?

DAVID. Don't you see, John, now that you're going away, and now that Joan's dead, I haven't anybody in the world except Helen. I can't let her go. I can't.

JOHN. No, of course you can't. I quite see that.

WILLIAMS *comes in.*

WILLIAMS. (*To* JOHN.) Your taxi is here, sir.

JOHN. What about my bags?

WILLIAMS. The porter's putting them on the taxi now, sir.

JOHN. Good.

WILLIAMS. I found this in the bathroom, sir. Does it belong to you? (*He produces a celluloid duck.*)

JOHN. Yes. I'll put it in my coat pocket. Thanks.

WILLIAMS *goes out.*

Well, I suppose I've got to go off to that bloody town. Goodbye, David.

DAVID. I'm sorry you're going.

JOHN. So am I.

DAVID. I've got used to that fat shape on the sofa.

JOHN. And I've got used to that sofa. It's quite a wrench to leave it.

DAVID. I'm sorry I shouted at you a moment ago.

JOHN. That's all right. It's not the first time I've been ordered to leave the house.

DAVID. No, it's not, is it?

JOHN. It's funny I should actually be leaving the house, isn't it?

DAVID. It doesn't seem possible.

JOHN. Well, goodbye.

DAVID. I'll come downstairs.

JOHN. No, don't do that. I won't be able to think of anything to say, and we'll probably shock the hall porter by bursting into tears.

DAVID. Goodbye.

They shake hands.

JOHN. I'll send you a coloured postcard of the town hall.

DAVID. I'd love that. Hurry up or you'll miss the train.

JOHN. I mustn't do that. It's got a restaurant car, and I've every intention of seeing Manchester for the first time through a mist of alcohol. Oh, God, why am I doing this?

He goes out.

DAVID, *left alone, wanders around aimlessly. He picks up one of the London Library books, glances through it and throws it down on the sofa. It is getting dark.* DAVID *goes to the window, hesitates a moment and then steps out on to the balcony. As if making a terrific effort, he slowly leans over and looks down. He stays in that position for a few seconds and then steps back into the room, closing the window after him.*

WILLIAMS *comes in.*

WILLIAMS. Excuse me, sir.

DAVID *looks round slowly.*

DAVID. What?

WILLIAMS. Are you dining in or out tonight, sir?

DAVID. In, Williams.

WILLIAMS. Yes, sir. How many?

DAVID. Two. Just myself and Miss Potter.

WILLIAMS. Thank you, sir.

DAVID. Oh, Williams.

WILLIAMS. Yes, sir?

DAVID. Do you know Joseph's Restaurant?

WILLIAMS. Yes, sir.

DAVID. I'll want you to take a letter round there at half-past seven to Miss Banner; and Williams – pack.

WILLIAMS. Pack, sir?

DAVID. Yes, Williams, pack. I'm going away tomorrow.

WILLIAMS. Very good, sir.

He goes out.

DAVID *quickly draws all the curtains and turns on the lamp by the piano; then, on an impulse, looks up a private number in a private book, picks up the telephone and dials. He strums four notes of 'Avalon' as he waits for a reply.*

Hello, Moya . . . David . . . David . . . Yes, I can hear it. It sounds like a good party. Listen, is Peter there? Well, stop him, will you? . . . Wait a minute. Don't tell him it's me . . . All right . . . Peter . . . Don't ring off, this is important . . . Listen, damn you, let me speak . . . I'm not going to lecture you. I've got some news that might interest you, that's all . . . I can't tell you what it is now, but you'll hear about it all right in time. Listen, Peter, will you promise me you won't cut your date with Helen tomorrow? It's important . . . No, I'm not joking . . . it's really important both for you and for her . . . Promise me . . . Thank you . . . Yes, that's all . . . Get Moya back, will you? . . . Hello, Moya! Listen. What are you doing after dinner? . . . Will it, that's grand. Then I'll come round . . . Who's there? All the old crowd, I suppose . . . No, I can't come over now. I've got a letter to write that's going to take hours . . . Yes, I'd love to, later . . . I'll be feeling lonely.

He rings off, and then very slowly reaches for the whisky decanter, and pulls it towards him.

Curtain.

Josie